i am weak

BUT HE

IS

STRONG

i am weak

But He

Is Strong

Fight Spiritually and Win

Kim Irby, MHL, BSN, RNC

Sweet Cherry Blossoms Press

i am weak But He Is Strong

Sweet Cherry Blossoms
Press

P.O. Box 533
Kannapolis, NC 28082
ISBN:
Paperback: 979-8-218-36966-8
Hardcover: 979-8-218-40222-8
Library of Congress Control
Number: TXu002-426-406

Table of Contents

Dedication

I want to dedicate this book to my husband, Scott. He tolerated me for twenty years while I lived with my feet planted firmly in all things of this world. He was saved when I met him. He took me to church for twenty years. I did not want to go but would go to appease him. He never gave up on me. For that, I have heartfelt gratitude. I would also like to dedicate this book to my children, Kailey, Peyton, and Jacob. They were raised by a woman who was corrupted by this world. A hateful, vile woman who had little patience and who was quick to yell to solve problems. You all turned out great despite me. Thank you so much for tolerating me. I love you all. If this book speaks to one soul, it was all worth the effort. The enemy wants to make sure we do not discover the truth and find the hidden gem that is Jesus Christ.

What People Are Saying About
i am weak But He Is Strong

"This book is awesome, and I believe it will touch many souls. I can see the passion throughout this book, and I believe it is anointed."

-Pastor Flip Benham

"It is truly inspiring and life-changing. I was saved after reading this book! My heart changed. I found the best-kept secret of this life."

-Summer Buchanan, my niece
This book was written for family

"'I am weak, But He Is Strong' is a profound and moving testament to the transformative power of faith. This testimony provides hope for anyone struggling with addiction, offering a compelling narrative of overcoming life's deepest valleys through the strength found in Jesus Christ. Packed with scriptural wisdom, this book illuminates the path from darkness to light, showcasing the life-saving power of surrendering to God's grace. A must-read for anyone seeking renewal and strength through Christian principles. You, too, can win!"

-Pastor Charles Church

"All I can say is WOW! This book will touch many faithful and unfaithful. You do such a terrific job combining your experience, thoughts, and verses. I am truly touched, and I am so proud of you."

-David Hopkins, my stepfather
This book was written for family

Mark 16:17
These miraculous signs will accompany those who believe: They will cast out demons in my name, and they will speak in new languages.

Ephesians6:11-12
Put on all of God's armor so that you will be able to stand firm against all the strategies of the devil. For we do not wrestle against flesh and blood, but against principalities, against powers, against the rulers of the darkness of this world, against spiritual wickedness in high places.

Acts10:38
And you know that God anointed Jesus of Nazareth with the Holy Spirit and with power. Then Jesus went around doing good and healing all who were oppressed by the devil, for God was with Him.

Matthew10:8
Heal the sick, raise the dead, cure those with leprosy, and cast out demons. Give as freely as you have received.

Matthew12:22
Then, a demon-possessed man, who was blind and couldn't speak, was brought to Jesus. He healed the man so that he could both speak and see.

Luke 10:17
When the seventy-two disciples returned, they joyfully reported to him, "Lord, even the demons obey us when we use your name!"

James 2:19
You say you have faith, for you believe that there is one God. Good for you! Even the demons believe this, and they tremble in terror.

John 3:16-17
For this is how God loved the world: He gave His one and only Son, so that everyone who believes in him will not perish but have eternal life. God sent his Son into the world not to judge the world, but to save the world through him.

Mark 5:9
Then Jesus demanded, "What is your name?" And he replied, "My name is Legion, because there are many of us inside this man."

Acts 5:16
Crowds came from the villages around Jerusalem, bringing their sick and those possessed by evil spirits, and they were all healed.

Preface

We can all agree that we are in a spiritual war like we have never seen before. I authored this book for two reasons. I want to help lead unbelievers to the foot of the cross so they may walk free like me. Secondly, to help saved Christians realize their power and authority. Many churches give a watered-down version of these truths. Please keep reading to find answers to many questions I have had over the years as a pretend Christian. When my eyes were opened, I chased the questions until I found the answers.

In this book, you will frequently see the words "Jesus" and "demon." Jesus is how we fight demons. Do you notice how both these words make people uncomfortable? Have you ever asked yourself why?

You will see things repeatedly. They were deliberately left because a demon will distract you from seeing and hearing the truth. If you were distracted the first time you read it, the demon may slip up and allow you to see it the second time.

These words are not meant to judge but to warn and give fighting tools. We all sin and fall short. I committed many of the sins spoken about in this book myself. Sin is how the enemy attacks us. Each sin comes with its own style of attack from the enemy. This book intends to teach how we are attacked through sin and how to fight back.

This book will feel like a biography to begin with, but that is not its purpose. I had to explain how I knew what I knew. The reader needed to know what urged me to read and study everything I could find about the spirit realm and fighting demons by speaking the name of Jesus.

When I woke up each morning, thoughts would come into my head. These thoughts were not articulated in a way that I could communicate. I began writing them down and realized I needed to share them with others.

Once I surrendered to Jesus Christ, I was saved and found this life's best secret. I would not trust Him previously because I thought I would have to stop living as I was. The beauty of Jesus is that He changes your life for you once you trust Him.

When all your thoughts change, your life changes. When He steps in, your heart's desires change, and your mind changes about everything. You become content living a life with a decreased need to sin. You do not decide to make better decisions. The Holy Spirit guides you and helps you to make better decisions. Your life begins to feel peaceful, and you are filled with joy. You begin to have patience, self-control, understanding, wisdom, gentleness, love, and goodness. Sin steals all those things. You feel you have nothing to prove to anyone on this earth anymore. The best way I can describe it is walking free.

I realized we are all in an unseen war with evil every minute of every day. Our decisions, actions, words, practices, and habits give the enemy the right to attack us. When we blame God for terrible things, we put the blame in the wrong place. Look at our own lives and determine what sins we are committing that give demons the right to attack us. Blame the devil for attacking you, not God Almighty.

Children and babies are attacked because of their parents' and ancestors' sins. It is a tough pill to swallow. When you realize how unseen enemies attack you, you can take steps to foil their plans against you and your descendants!

Many Christians fear speaking about demons. They believe it will increase the chances they will be attacked. We have power over them by speaking the name of Jesus. Talking about demons is not what brings them to attack you. Your "yes" is what makes them attack you. When you give sin a "yes," you are giving the keys of your life to demons. You are opening the door and welcoming them in to kill, steal, and destroy you. Your decisions make deals with the devil. He will take way more than he ever gave you.

This book is a "how to" on protecting yourself and your family from the enemy. Learn how to fight effectively in the spirit and overcome the devil's plans for your life and the lives of your descendants. Step into your authority and protect yourself and your entire bloodline.

Warning

If you use any advice in this book to cast out demons, understand that you must invite the Holy Spirit into your heart first by asking Jesus to save you from this life with your mouth and heart. *Matthew 12:43-45*

43When an evil spirit leaves a person, it goes into the desert, seeking rest but finding none. 44 Then it says, "I will return to the person I came from." So, it returns and finds its former home empty, swept, and in order. 45 Then the spirit finds seven other spirits more evil than itself, and they all enter the person and live there. And so that person is worse off than before. That will be the experience of this evil generation."

When you invite Jesus, the Holy Spirit will dwell in your heart, and the demons spoken about in

Matthew 12:43-45 will not find the house vacant. When the Holy Spirit lives in your heart, the demons cannot enter. In conjunction with Jesus and God Almighty, the Holy Spirit places a hedge of heavenly protection over you that the demons cannot break. You will then be adopted into the kingdom of heaven, your name will be written in The Book of Life, and all the powers spoken about in this book will be yours!

The spirit realm is real; if you attempt to access it through anyone other than the Holy Spirit, you are dealing with demons. Demons only seek to kill, steal, and destroy your life, the lives of your family, and your descendants.

Have you done something or said something that you are not proud of? Have you ever thought God could never forgive you for what you did and said? Are you living enslaved to addiction? Are you living under the curse of fear, depression, and anxiety? Watch those things fall to your feet!

Believe me when I tell you I have done and said some horrific things in my life. I lived in addiction for a long time. I knew I did not deserve to be forgiven for the plethora of evil things I had done and said over the years. But when I could not take this life anymore, I cried out to Jesus in the middle of the storm. He reached down and changed my whole life around. He not only saved my soul from eternal damnation, but He made this life so much sweeter! Do you want the freedom I have found?

Speak this aloud and with your heart with sincerity:
Dear Father in Heaven, I admit that I am a sinner. I have done many things that do not please you. I have lived my life for myself only. I am sorry, and I repent. I ask you to forgive me. I forgive anyone who has ever wronged me, just as I want you to forgive me now.
I believe you sent your Son, Jesus, to die on the cross for me to save me from this life and pay for all the sins I have committed. You did what I could not do for myself. I come to you now and ask you to take control of my life; I give it to you.

From this day forward, help me live every day for you and in a way that pleases you. I love you, Lord, and thank you for allowing me to spend all eternity in heaven with you. Amen

Side note: You must continue to seek Jesus every day. Seek His counsel, love, and peace. Watch what happens in your life!

Speak this aloud with
authority every time you sit
to read this book:

Unclean spirits, attempting to keep
me from knowing the truth, I take
spiritual authority over you in the
mighty name of Jesus. I silence,
muzzle, and quiet you while reading
this book in Jesus' name.
This is not a compromise; this is a
command. You have no authority here!
Holy Spirit, please guide me while I
read this book. Help me to see and
hear the truth in Jesus's precious
name.
Amen.

Chapter 1

Saved? What Does That Mean?

I was an alcoholic for thirty-five years. I smoked cigarettes whenever I drank. I often smoked a whole pack of cigarettes in one episode of drinking to get drunk. When I was sixteen, I was drinking at a party and drove home. When I left there, I got a ticket for DWI. I lost my license for a year. I would use any excuse to get drunk. Did something good happen? Get drunk! Did something terrible happen? Get drunk! Is it Friday? Get drunk! You don't have to drink every day to be an alcoholic. It was my mind that was consumed by it. It was my evil master. I would wake up each morning and wonder if today was a day that I could sit and get drunk for those thirty- five years. I would think about the next time I planned to get drunk. It was like a job. When you are an alcoholic, you wake up feeling drained and hungover the following day. It consumes your life. When you go somewhere, you must know if alcohol will be served there. You cannot drive yourself anywhere because you know you plan to get drunk. You sleep in places you did not plan to sleep. Sometimes, you plan to stay home and drink to avoid spending money getting expensive drinks somewhere. Your life becomes consumed and ruled by alcohol. Alcohol is the first thing that helps you make decisions on what you will do today, tomorrow, or the weekend. It then becomes a never-ending cycle.

You also say things you would have normally kept to yourself when you are drinking. A sober man's thoughts are a drunk man's words. I used to feel ashamed when someone called the following day and said, "Do you remember saying _____ last night?" or "Do you remember what you did last night?" I am sharing this because

I want you to know where I came from and where I am now.

When I planned to drink, I would make sure I had enough alcohol to get drunk. If anyone asked for something I was drinking, I would think to myself, "I bought just enough for me to get drunk." I began to buy extra alcohol in case anyone asked me for some of mine. If I were drinking and ran out of alcohol, I would find any way possible to get alcohol brought to me. If I ran out of cigarettes while I was drinking, I would also do anything to get more. I even had a pizza delivery man stop to get me cigarettes. I would go to a restaurant and drink a glass or two of wine. I would always have to come home and drink more until I was drunk and passed out. It was like being held hostage by someone! As I later found out, that is precisely what was happening. Demons were ruling my thoughts.

I was a liar, cheater, thief, self-centered, suicidal, and generally a bad person. People who know me may say, "You weren't a bad person at all." They did not know what was in my mind and heart. I would say I loved people when, in fact, I only loved myself. When I was truly saved, I

3

stopped drinking without even trying (2 years now), I stopped smoking cigarettes, I stopped taking antidepressants that I had taken for twenty-five years, and I went from the biggest slob to a clean person. I did not go to an Alcoholics Anonymous (AA) meeting or receive one chip for being sober. How? You may ask. I was saved by Jesus when I trusted Him. This is what it means to be saved. He saves you in every way. He saves this life you are living, and your soul is saved from living eternity in hell. This is why it is called being reborn when you are saved. That person you were is now dead and gone. You become a new creation. I went to church for twenty years with my husband, who was saved. I just recently found out my husband was a drinker and lived a life that looked vastly different than it looks now. I met him just two years after he was saved. He did not drink or enjoy going to parties. I began to think, "This is great; I have a driver." He drove me to many places over the twenty years while I was drunk. After being saved, I asked him why he had never told me this would happen. He said, "You wouldn't have believed me." I wonder if I was sent to him by God or the devil! Once you are saved, the devil works hard to get you back into that life. My husband stuck by me and endured a lot over those twenty years. What the devil means for evil God turns to good. I love him more now because I know what love is. I see what is in his heart, and I love him for that. I asked him if he would rather have that party girl back. He answers with a very stern, "No!" You see, my life, too, looks vastly different than before.

When I went to church, I was often hungover, snoring, and daydreaming. I just checked off the "We went to church" box. I went to appease my husband. Most of the time, I was daydreaming about what I would have for lunch, something I had to do tomorrow, or anything but what they were discussing. This is because the enemy keeps us distracted so that we will continue down the path of destruction.

I would not have shared this information with anyone while living that way. I was suicidal. Many times, I contemplated how I would kill myself. I would wonder what the most pain-free way out of this life was. I lied to myself by saying,

"My family will be better off without me." I thought that if I could just find an easy way to kill myself, this nightmare would be over for good. I stopped having suicidal thoughts and drinking altogether without trying. When I surrendered everything to Jesus Christ, He did it for me. Was I still an alcoholic and suicidal when I surrendered to Him? Yes, I was. He said I did not have to live enslaved to alcohol anymore. He pulled me out of that life and changed all my heart's desires. He cut those chains off, and they fell at my feet. I walked free.

I suppose many people believe you must go to church to be saved. People know going to church is something we should all do, but do they know why? You will be saved when you finally decide you have had enough of this life and ask Jesus to tap you out! You do not have to be in a particular building for that to happen. Going to church is so that you can be in the presence of the body of Christ. The body of Christ is the group of people who have been saved and born again. When you come together as one, there is power. This power gives you the energy and strength to live the week ahead.

I was not in church when I got saved. But I cannot get enough of it now. I love to be amongst the body of Christ. I hang on to every word because I now know the truth. I got saved when I was in my bedroom. I fell to my knees, reached my hands high above my head, and shouted Jesus, save me from this life! I did not want to be alive any longer. I said, "Did you put me on this earth to be a slave five days a week and have two days to myself?" Those two days were spent getting drunk at night and then starting all over again. I was fed up with struggling for everything I had since I was sixteen.

He reached down and saved me. He changed my thoughts about everything. Once I asked Him to save me with my mouth and heart, He stepped in and did just that. I had asked Him aloud to save me many times before when they would tell me to say the salvation prayer. No change happened until I also meant it with my heart. I was a pretend Christian.

I have seen others who have said the prayer to be saved but did not get the same change that happened to me. You must truly mean it from your heart. If you do not mean it, God will know. I know that once you ask Him with your mouth and heart, you must keep saying "yes" to Jesus. You must continue to seek Him each day. This is when the change occurs. This change is not something you have done on your own. The Holy Spirit steps in and changes your thoughts, your heart's desires, and your attitude toward everything. You suddenly become comfortable, at peace, satisfied, and joyful.

I suffered three strokes throughout my life. The first one was at the ripe old age of twenty-six. Did I stop smoking and drinking after rehab for those strokes? No. It appears that would have been motivation enough. I could not stop. I lost hearing in my right ear after the first stroke. I had to learn to walk, talk, and write again after my second stroke. Once my functioning came back four months later, I began to drink and smoke again! I still suffer from residual effects due to those strokes. Each time I get sick, stressed, or anxious, my stroke symptoms come back. I must go to the ER and spend a few days in the hospital. I get confused, cannot speak correctly, and cannot walk. It is the life I live now. The only difference is that I now have the peace and patience of the Holy Spirit.

People say, "Don't pray for patience." That is a lie from hell. When the Holy Spirit steps in, He brings patience, joy, love, peace, kindness, gentleness, and self-control. The Holy Spirit grants it to you. There is no feeling in the world like it. Your whole life transforms for the good.

We all expect Prince Charming to save us from this life. Nicole Johnson's book, "Keeping a Princess Heart," explains how a woman will think a knight in shining armor will come to rescue her from the tower. It is what is taught our whole lives through movies and fairy tales. The dragon has her held captive. When we learn to trust Jesus, He does just that. He saves us from the dragon (demons) who has control of our lives.

Truly asking Jesus to save you grants you passage to heaven and makes this life more bearable. I finally felt what love was for the first time in my life. Had I told people I loved them before? Yes, but I only knew what that meant or felt like once I was saved. I thought it meant I enjoyed their company and wanted to spend time with them.

When you genuinely love someone, you want what is best for them. You genuinely want them to have their heart's desires.

I feel so much compassion for those still living their life, thinking they know what love is when they have never experienced the true love that Jesus Christ brings to their life. You learn what love is for the first time in your life. You suddenly feel love and compassion for strangers. When I see a homeless person, I feel that it is a friend of mine who is standing there with no food or shelter. Would you stop and help a friend of yours if you saw them in that situation?

When they talked about asking Jesus to be my Lord and Savior in church, I did not know what it was all about. I had gone to church so long that I thought I would look foolish asking. He truly does save you from this life! You feel forgiven for everything you did previously in your life. Peace, joy, love, and hope wash over you. It covers you like a blanket, making you feel warm and safe for the first time.

You go from thinking certain things are true to knowing the truth. In my pretend Christian life, I was selfish and couldn't care less if I saw someone in need. I may stop and give them food or a little money. I was quick to tell someone so that I would look like a good person. Once you are saved, you do not feel the pressing need to tell someone what you have done to prove to them what a worthwhile person you are. You now only have one person to please: God Almighty. You do that because you know beyond doubt that He is watching everything you do. You want nothing more than to please Him. You find yourself doing things you know will make God's heart smile. He wants us to take care of each other. I dreamed I was talking to a blonde-headed man dressed in white. I could ask him any question I had. I asked, "Are we here to help each other get back home?" He grinned at me and said, "You're on the right path." I said, "I knew it! Ever since Jesus saved me, I have wanted to help others. The closer I get to God, the stronger the feeling gets."

You also begin to realize there is absolutely a heaven and a hell. Everything you have been told about heaven and hell begins to make sense. You know you have been adopted into God's kingdom. You begin to realize you are not merely

God's creation anymore, but you are now a child of God, bought and paid for at the foot of the cross by the blood of Jesus.

The rewards of heaven will be so sweet once we leave this world. Demons do not reside in heaven, so no one can cause us pain, suffering, or sorrow. We will live in complete bliss. We will see our Christian loved ones that have passed. We will enjoy our dream houses. Streets will be lined with gold. Heaven is a place of great beauty. When we are in heaven, we will have no memory of loved ones who did not make it. I previously did not give much thought to heaven, but now I cannot wait! Many pastors say that if you say this prayer, you are saved. "Jesus, come into my heart. Forgive my sin. I make you the Lord and Savior of my life." I said that prayer many times over the years. I did not know what that meant, so how could I mean it with my heart? But after I said it, I thought I was saved, which seemed important. I thought I was saved and safe from eternal damnation and fire because I had spoken that phrase aloud. I was not saved at all.

I believe many pastors do not have ill intentions or mean to lead people astray. However, if they don't express the part about meaning it with your heart, they are doing just that. I do not blame them, however. I blame the devil for distracting me so I couldn't hear and understand the truth. There is more to it than just speaking the prayer. You must speak it from the heart, with heartfelt repentance and a deep desire for personal change. People will say, "I was baptized, so I am saved," or "I went to the altar at church and prayed, so I am saved." They will also say," I'm a good person," or "I give to charities," or "I feed the homeless," so surely, I am going to heaven. These things do not make you saved any more than sitting in a garage makes you a car.

Suppose you went to court for a crime. The judge asks how you plead, and you say, "I'm a good person, so surely you will let me go." That seems absurd, but that's how people think the kingdom of heaven works. They think they will go to heaven if they are a good person. Think of it as a crime you have committed for which you cannot pay. Jesus stepped in and paid the price for our sins. All we must do is believe in Him and accept the gift of forgiveness and salvation. We still owe the fee for our sins if we do not accept Him. We cannot pay for these sins on our own. Let me rephrase that. You will eventually pay for these sins when you die and go to hell for eternity. When Christians speak of the "change" or the "new creation," they are not speaking of any change they did. In conjunction with Jesus and God Almighty, the Holy Spirit does all the changing for us. It is not a decision to change. You must only trust Jesus to save you, repent (or say you are sorry and turn from that sin) for your sins, forgive everyone, ask Him to save you, and trust Him to save you. Sit back and watch your life change in ways you could have never imagined.

I would not trust Jesus entirely for most of the years of my life because I thought I would have to stop drinking for Him to accept me. He accepted me just like I was! He gave me the gift of this new life once I trusted Him. I have so much compassion for those who do not know Him or those who have not accepted Him. What a hard life that was. The song lyrics of "Already Gone" by the Eagles come to mind: "We live our lives in chains, never even knowing we have the keys." This sums it up perfectly.

People who say they were saved multiple times are probably still not saved. I say this because if they think they were saved the first two times and the third time, they do not know how it feels to be saved. If you did not have a change that happened in your heart, you were not saved. Jesus knows your heart. He knows if you have not truly surrendered to Him. He knows if you still hold resentment towards someone who wronged you. You must forgive others so that Jesus will forgive you for the sins you have committed. It is imperative to say aloud and with your heart, "I forgive _____ for_____. Just as I want you to forgive me now, Jesus." You want Jesus to forgive you and cancel your debt, right? You must forgive everyone for what they have done to you. The Lord's Prayer says to forgive others for trespasses as you want the Lord to forgive your trespasses. It says we must forgive others if we want God to forgive us. This is key to salvation.

You are not saved if you think you are saved, yet you have not changed by no doing of your own. When you are saved, you see the world through a different lens. All your heart's desires change. Satan has put many pitfalls in this life to deceive people into believing they are saved when they are not. He adds confusion around salvation. For example, when I was too afraid to ask what it meant to be saved. I thought I was saved for many years because I said the prayer.

Something called "backsliding" will make you question your salvation. This is after you have already had the change and consciously decided to return to that life. If you decide to do that, each foot you put into sin takes you one step away from God. You leave peace, joy, patience, love, wisdom, understanding, and self-control. The devil will see you as a tasty morsel because he loves to make God's children stumble. He will take every opportunity to destroy you because you have turned your back on God and the protection He provides. Even after you know there is a loving God in heaven, you do not choose to follow Him.

When you have struggles in life, you can choose one of two paths. You can choose bitterness, hatred, and anger, or you can choose to look up and cry aloud to Jesus to save you from this life.

Misinterpreting baptism is one of the pitfalls Satan sends. Let me elaborate. The Bible does say you are to be baptized to enter the gates of heaven. *Mark 16:16* says, "Whoever believes and is baptized will be saved, but whoever does not believe will be condemned." People are deceived into believing they are saved by baptism alone. They believe they are saved when they come out of the water and the new creation that real saved Christians talk about. This is untrue. Baptism is a public declaration of something that happened to you in private. If you are not saved in the Spirit, baptism is just someone dunking another person underwater.

I have known people who got baptized two or three times, and no change happened. A change they themselves did not make. Once they trusted

Jesus and got water baptized, they were truly saved and baptized. Their name was written in the Lamb's Book of Life.

My mother says her father would get into arguments with people about baptism. I searched my heart about why someone would be so against baptism when it is clearly written in the Bible. I realized he saw people getting baptized and thinking they were saved. The danger with someone thinking they are saved is that they stop searching and seeking a relationship with Jesus. I told someone I stopped drinking because I was saved. He said, "What do you mean? You were baptized?" This shows what people think baptism is. Again, these are deceptions of Satan. Should you get baptized after you are saved? Absolutely, just do not get baptized without first being saved.

Once you are saved, Jesus will baptize you in the Holy Spirit. This is when the Holy Spirit comes to live in you. He helps guide you and light your path. He gives you an understanding of things you previously did not even think about.

Many unbelievers want to say, "If there is a God, then why does he let_____happen?"

Oh, I was one of them. I would get into arguments with people. I would skeptically tell them to give me proof that there is a God. They would stare at me and give me what I thought were lame answers. I was in my early twenties and thought I knew everything. If someone says that to me now, I have much to say! I mean, I wrote a book on the subject.

People blame God for what the devil does. When we sin, we give Satan the keys to our lives. We allow him to come in and wreak havoc. Then, when all this havoc happens, we blame God for allowing it. Let me tell you, we allow it by sinning and giving Satan rights over our lives. When you choose Jesus, He sends the Holy Spirit to live in you. He will allow you to live your life without the chains of sin. Do you still sin? Yes, we are all sinners. You begin to feel bad when you sin. You try not to because you love and fear God. The kind of fear I am speaking about is the fear that you will disappoint Him. You begin to love God with your entire heart and speak to Him throughout the day. After you initially surrender your heart, you must keep seeking His face. As I said, you must continue to say "yes" to Jesus daily. Watch chains of strongholds fall at your feet.

When Jesus saved me, I realized I did not have to work so hard for the biggest house, the nicest car, or any possession I thought might impress someone. I always tried to fool everyone into thinking I had it all together. But now, I was finally happy with what I already had. I even felt that I had excess. It is like a different person took over my body. A person who no longer enjoys sin. A person who is not impressed by all the things of this world.

People think, "It would be hard to follow Jesus because you have to live a sin-free life." It is not hard because He lays that down for you. It is not a daily struggle because He removes the desire to sin. Do you still sin? Yes, but the difference is that when you do, you immediately become disgusted with yourself and ask for forgiveness. You feel very ashamed of what you have done. You want to live a life that makes your Father in heaven happy.

I thought that for those thirty-five years I was living in slavery to alcohol, I would have to give up drinking if I truly surrendered to Jesus, but I did not know how I would do that. That is the good news when you surrender. He lays it down for you. I gave up drinking in the blink of an eye. As I previously stated, I did not go to one Alcoholics Anonymous meeting or receive a chip for being sober. He said I did not have to live in slavery to addiction any longer. He traded my old rags for riches. It was metaphorically going from being homeless to moving into a beautiful mansion.

Life is so much sweeter on this side of the fence. It is the biggest kept secret of this life. If someone offered me all the money in the world to return to my life before I was saved, I would not take it. People see my life as different but think I decided to be different. But the Holy Spirit now lives in me and makes me different. It is fantastic!

Selah

The church was doing what is called Selah. This started the year with a fast. I did not know how I would do the fast because it was all I could think about, even if I missed one meal. The fast is a time to draw closer to God through prayer. The night before the fast, I said aloud to Jesus, "How will I ever be able to fast even one day? I think about you all day, but I am afraid if I do not eat, my mind will go from you to food."

I was not as hungry as usual when I woke up the next day. I was able to go the entire day without being hungry. I prayed and talked to Jesus all day. Then, day two came, and it was the same thing. On day three, I decided not to drink water either. I went for four more days without food or water. Two weeks went by without food.

I sat at tables in nice restaurants with my family, even my extended family. I was not eating a bite of the delicious food on the table, and all the time, I was praying for the salvation of their souls. You see, I realize there is heaven and hell, and I cannot bear the thought of any of my family going there. I thought they would believe me when I told them what happened to me, but they could not hear what I was saying because the enemy bombarded their thoughts with evil, lies, and distractions. I felt as though I was standing in a room screaming, and no one could hear me.

I know that going for two weeks without food was not my doing. Jesus allowed me to do that, and He made that possible, not me. *Matthew 17:21* says, "However, this kind does not come out except by prayer and fasting." This refers to certain demons that have strongholds on people. I will speak later about demons and the truths I have learned.

I do realize the Bible says you should not tell people you are fasting. However, we should speak to each other about it because many people do not understand what they should do. Didn't Moses tell the people when he came down from the mountain that he fasted for 40 days? How did people know Jesus fasted for 40 days? They had to tell the people after the fact. The scriptures speak about telling people you are fasting while you are fasting. When you give the glory to God, you are not lifting yourself on a pedestal. You are giving God the credit. It becomes a testimony after you have completed it. You are not supposed to act sad and depressed while you are fasting. The enemy wants to ensure we do not discuss it so that we do not encourage each other to fast.

Fasting resets our physical and spiritual bodies. Our food contains many things that are not healthy for us. Give fasting a try and seek Jesus; you will see spiritual breakthroughs.

Comparison is the Thief of Joy

When I lived with my feet firmly planted in all things of this world, I constantly looked at others' appearances. I would think, "Wow, that guy looks good!" or "Man, that woman is pretty!" I do not care about any of that anymore. The heart of someone is the only thing I look to and try hard to see. When someone has a heart for others and compassion for strangers, my heart leaps out of my chest.

We struggle our whole life to keep up with the Joneses. Life is a contest about who has the best stuff, right? Wrong! This is a lie the enemy tells us to ensure we squander the money we have been given. We will always be enslaved because we are in a perpetual loop of struggling for money and spending time impressing others. If we practice giving our first ten percent in the name of Jesus, financial blessings will chase us down. When I see people trying so hard to impress others with what they have, I look at them compassionately. They are struggling so hard to collect stuff. This life is temporary. Everything you collect will not be useful when your flesh dies away.

Believe me when I say there is life in the spirit after your flesh is gone. There is a secret to having everything your heart desires: believing you already have it. When Jesus changed my brain, He made me believe I already had everything. Now, I live a life full of blessings beyond my wildest imagination! I remember to thank God throughout the day for each of these things. I mean sincere gratitude. I am not just saying it because it is a good idea but because I have heartfelt gratitude. Try this practice. It is life-changing.

Near Death Experience

There was a documentary about people who

died and went to heaven. It is called "Life to Afterlife Death and Back." One person said God showed her life on a screen in the sky. She was so fearful because all she could think about was all the dreadful things she had done. To her surprise, the movie was about all the good milestones in her life. These are the points in life people consider to be reasons to celebrate or look at you with admiration. Such as awards she received, graduating college, and getting a fantastic job. He then had her put on glasses and watch again. This time, the only things that played were when she showed someone compassion, love, and understanding.

I realized this was God's heart because I felt the same way once I was saved. Suddenly, I was not impressed by everything people considered to be a success. I was only impressed and filled with joy when people showed compassion, love, and understanding for someone. I began to see people by only looking at their hearts. I had no interest in the clothes they wore, the car they drove, or the house where they lived. I had no interest in their appearance, education, or job. I only waited to see what was in their heart. You can see what is in someone's heart by what they say, where they go, what they do, what they look at, and what they listen to. What they allow into their body through the eyes and ears is a good indicator of where their heart lives. But the best indicator is their tongue. Listen, and people will tell you who they are, whether they know they are doing it or not.

In *Matthew 15:11,* Jesus said, "What goes into someone's mouth does not defile them, but what comes out of their mouth, that is what defiles them." Our tongues are powerful. Guard your words. Are you speaking life or death over yourself? What about your children? What about your spouse?

When I saw the woman talking in the documentary about how the Father loves us, I thought that is God's heart and how He views the world. His heart is sorrowful when we pursue anything that people consider impressive while stepping on others to achieve that. It also makes His heart sad when we view this world's achievements as a success while ignoring the real success of life. Faith, love, hope, peace, joy, patience, self-control, understanding, and having a heart for others are the true successes of this life—not money or stuff. You will understand this once you accept Jesus into your heart and the Holy Spirit comes to live in you. Unfortunately, most people will never see or feel that. God made us with these things in our hearts. The world corrupted us into believing the lie.

It is challenging to lead others to the foot of the cross because they cannot see or hear these truths. They will not understand until they surrender to God through Jesus Christ. The veil will remain over their eyes until they believe what is true.

Asbury

My heart was stirred to travel to a spontaneous revival alone. A school in Wilmore, Kentucky, called Asbury University, was having a revival that started from a regular praise and worship meeting. The revival had been going on for seven days straight. The college students had been worshipping twenty-four hours a day for seven days!

I woke on Wednesday morning, day seven of two weeks, and said, "I have to get there." I drove by myself for six and a half hours one way through the mountains of Kentucky (I do not usually like to drive through the mountains). There was a particular chapel where the revival was taking place. It was called Hughes Auditorium. I was able to walk straight into the auditorium where the revival was. You could feel the Holy Spirit moving there. A feeling of peace was in the whole place. I walked straight to the altar, went to my knees, and cried tears that streamed down my face. After leaving the altar, I sat next to Regina a few rows back. She said she was from Asbury and asked where I was from. I told her I had just arrived thirty minutes ago after driving six and a half hours. I was only able to stay one more hour. I picked up my coat and said, "I have to go." She said, "You just got here!" She asked if I wanted them to pray for me. I told her, "Yes, I have been a horrible person. I raised my daughter, Peyton, and did not know Jesus." I told her I was different now because Jesus had changed me. My oldest daughter, Kailey, and stepson,

Jacob had already been saved and baptized as teenagers, and they went on mission trips. But my fear was for Peyton because she had not yet found salvation. I blamed myself.

A group of five ladies surrounded me and prayed for Peyton's salvation. I left and drove another six and a half hours back home through the Kentucky mountains in the dark. Regina texted me the next day: "You do not know how much what you did affected me and the other people who prayed for you! We could not stop talking about it! What love you have for your daughter! Get ready, get ready, get ready. God is moving in Peyton's life! There is one thing you said that is lying in my heart. You said you have been an awful person in your past. God wants you to read *Romans 8:1.* 'There is now no condemnation to them which are in Christ Jesus, who walk not after the flesh, but after the Spirit' That person is dead and gone. I am so glad God sat you beside me!"

I drove thirteen hours that day and never once thought it was annoying. The drive itself was peaceful. I returned to Asbury on Sunday after church with my husband. The wait to get into Hughes Auditorium was three hours. First, we sat on the huge grassy area where large screens streamed from inside. It was cold, so we went to a chapel across the street with large screens streaming from Hughes. We did get into Hughes Auditorium that night, but not until 1 a.m. We stayed in a hotel and went back the next day. The wait to get into Hughes Auditorium was six hours. There were people lined up down the street and around the block.

The Holy Spirit was moving at that college. God is starting a worldwide revival. He wants to ensure He wins as many souls as possible before Jesus returns. Many Christians believe we are in the end times. Now is the time to seek Jesus!

This story came full circle when Peyton got baptized on December 31, 2023. My heart was filled with so much love and joy. Tears were streaming down my face. I felt I could leave this earth in peace because all my children had been saved and baptized. I knew I was responsible for leading them in this life and had done a crummy job. But God...

"Christian Concert"

I attended a huge "Christian concert" in downtown Charlotte a few months later. I went to the supposed Christian concert alone. When I got home, I felt like my heart had been used as a punching bag. Satan was there in a big way. Only two of the seven bands were Christian. The other bands claimed to be Christian but were not. They were rapping and screaming into the microphone. When I looked up the lyrics, they were indubitably not Christian. The chorus would slow down long enough to say, "Good Lord." This had everyone lulled into thinking God had anointed them. They were singing at a Christian concert, right?

There were many church buses outside the concert. This concert had everyone checking the box off, "I went to a Christian concert." God said, in *Hosea 4:6*, "My people are being destroyed because they don't know me. Since you priests refuse to know me, I refuse to recognize you as my priest. Since you have forgotten the laws of your

God, I will forget to bless your children." These types of things, I believe, are what He was referring to.

The band that came on last was also full of deception. They had the whole room dark and began shining red lights and lasers. The entire room was red. They had a massive snake on the screen that exploded. The guitar player started playing "The Chain" by Fleetwood Mac. This song's lyrics say- "Damn your love, damn your life. You will never break the chain." When you are saved, all your chains are broken. We never sang one song about snakes or the devil when I visited the Asbury Revival twice. Christian songs glorify Jesus. They do not talk about Satan.

I will share more about my spiritual journey with Jesus, the Holy Spirit, and Almighty God. I started reading the Bible each day and reflecting after reading it. I had a few hours left to finish reading it. I drove to the "Pretty Place" in Cleveland, SC, about two and a half hours from my house. It is an open chapel that looks out on an incredible mountain scene with a large cross. I sat there for four hours and completed my ten-month journey to read the Bible. When Jesus changed my heart, He added the love of reading. I find that to be amazing because in my life as a pretend Christian, I hated reading. I would rather zone out in front of the television. I only watch TV occasionally now and would much rather read. I used to think people who said that were weird. Now I know the joy of it.

I had only read two books my whole life. I have now read four books about spiritual warfare, five Christian books, and the entire Bible this past year! When I say read these books, I mean read for understanding. In college, I read books to take a test and restate the information. It was not to learn. I did not care about what I was reading. When I read, I read to learn and study the information. I have gained so much knowledge. I am more educated than I ever was because of a master's degree from college.

I was sitting at an Irish airport with my daughter and son-in-law. We were heading back home from a weeklong vacation to Ireland and Iceland. I was proofreading this book just before it was published. I began to weep because I was so thankful for this life I have now. Words cannot describe what my heart feels. As we landed in Ireland, I looked out the window, and tears welled up in my eyes—tears of joy. I would be able to enjoy my Ireland trip. In my pretend Christian life, I would have been worrying about where we would get drunk. I would have been drinking like it was my job. I would want to spend the next day in bed because of a horrendous hangover. I would have wanted to spend every minute and every dollar in an Irish Pub. However, i now know that i am weak, BUT HE IS STRONG!

Chapter 2

Fully Awake With a Duty to Warn

When you begin to speak to unbelievers about Jesus, you realize something. You realize that a veil is placed over their eyes and deafness is placed over their ears so that they are not able to see or hear the truth. 2 Corinthian 3:14 says, "But the people's minds were hardened, and to this day whenever the old covenant is being read, the same veil covers their minds so they cannot understand the truth. And this veil can be removed only by believing in Christ." I wish I had known this when I first set out to tell everyone what had actually happened to me. I was astounded when they would change the subject or act as if I had just told them the steps of how my paint dried on the wall. It is an astounding story! No one batted an eyelash. The veil may be there so that no caterpillar comes out of their chrysalis too early. It upsets me to think the devil put it there, and they still ignore my proof of what Jesus did. Jesus said in *John 8:31-32,* "If you continue in My word, you are truly My disciples. Then you will know the truth, and the truth will set you free." The truth of Jesus Christ absolutely sets you free. Who the Son sets free is free indeed. How often have you heard, "The truth shall set you free?" I have always thought it meant telling the truth would take a burden off your shoulders, and you would feel set free from that lie. The Bible is talking about knowing the truth about Jesus, which will set you free. The only way to walk free is to ask Jesus with your mouth and heart to save you from this life. He will tap you out of the beating you have been taking this entire time. You will know Him, He will change your heart's desires, and you will walk free. Satan tries to distort all things from God to keep us living in distraction and confusion. He tries every trick he can to keep us from knowing the truth.

Again, there is absolutely a heaven and a hell. The cruelest trick the devil has played on humanity is convincing them he does not exist. People live their lives as if they will live forever. They do not want to hear what God has in store for this life and their eternal life.

The devil's slogan is "Do as thou whilst." Free will has people living this life as if they will live forever. I cannot caution everyone enough on the dangers of this. Free will is great, but God is a gentleman. He will never force His way into your life. He sits back with love and patience. Waiting for you to realize you need Him much more than stuff in this life. When you cry out to Him, watch your life undergo many transformations beyond your wildest dreams and expectations! *Mark 8:36-37* says, "And what do you benefit if you gain the whole world but lose your soul? Is anything worth more than your soul?"

I have compassion for those who have gained stuff and things in this life but will burn for eternity. Yet these people think they are deeply impressing people with their possessions. I am enamored by the people who are saved. They will be kings seated together with Christ. Jesus does not care about the things we own; He only cares that we steward what He has given us to build the kingdom of heaven. He only sees our hearts. We will be rewarded in heaven for the number of souls we lead to Him.

Works

Unbelievers will see saved Christians doing charitable acts and think that is how they, too, will be saved. The saved Christians do charitable acts because they are saved, not to become saved. Salvation comes, and then the charitable acts or works come. Works or good deeds will not save you. You must first be saved. Please understand this!

When you do good deeds, you must do them in Jesus' name. The Bible says you cannot be saved by works alone. However, wouldn't you love to build your mansion bigger in heaven by the works you do after you are saved? *Matthew*

6:20 says this: "But lay up for yourselves treasures in heaven, where neither moth nor rust destroys and where thieves do not break in and steal." This is how we lay up treasures in heaven. The good that God sees in secret, He will reward in public. As saved Christians, it is our job to bring others to the kingdom of heaven. Why would you not do everything you can for the gift you have been given? The more souls you lead to the foot of the cross, the more blessings you will have in eternity. Aside from that, imagine the people you lead to the foot of the cross that will then be saved from eternal damnation!

We must share this information with as many people as we can. I know Satan places a veil over their eyes and deafness over their ears so that they cannot see or hear the truth. But we can plant seeds in their minds. Cliff Knechtle sums it up exactly. Imagine you are taken away in the clouds and look back to see someone who says, "Hey, we were friends. We shared everything with each other. Why did you not share with me that Jesus would come, and this was how the world would end?" Imagine how bad you will feel when you have to say, "I didn't want you to think I was a Jesus freak or a religious nutcase." How selfish is that?

The devil tries hard to ensure we do not claim that mansion, which is becoming a born-again Christian, for ourselves. He wants to keep us homeless and desolate and our eyes on things of this world. I cannot say enough times that the devil only comes to kill, steal, and destroy our lives. He is terrified that people will trust in Jesus and forever have power over him.

The devil counterfeits everything God has sent to us. Witchcraft is the counterfeit of Christianity. Witchcraft calls on the power of demons, while Christianity calls on the power of the Holy Spirit and His angels. Are demons powerful? Absolutely! The Holy Spirit is, however, the most powerful. When you call on help from demons, they will collect a fee for their services. They will torment you and destroy your life. This book is designed to help Christians know their power and step into it by using the power of the Holy Spirit and speaking the name of Jesus.

Trusting in Jesus calls on power from the spirit realm. His power, however, is much stronger, and He controls the spiritual realm. The devil twists all things from the Holy Spirit to give people the illusion of power without Christ. Witchcraft requires you to speak spells, vexes, and incantations to gain power over another. These are asking demons for help. Demons will innocently enter your life. They will only leave with divine intervention once you invite them in by asking for their help.

Demons enter through a series of saying "yes" to them. Saying "yes" to sin is what brings them. To make them leave, you must close the door through which they originally came in. I will discuss this in more depth later. They will not leave without payment for their services. Payment through the destruction of your life.

Saved Christians also speak in power aloud. They are called spoken prayers and include "in Jesus' name" at the end of them! Add the words "in Jesus' name" to the end and watch what happens! When you speak His name with trust and love, He shows up in a big way. Trust in Jesus,

43

with all your heart and with all your mind. Speak it aloud! Speak to the hardships in your life: "Spirit of _____I cast you out in the name of Jesus. I am a child of God, bought and paid for at the foot of the cross, and you have no power in my life! I command you to leave in the name of Jesus!"

One of the biggest obstacles in our lives is fear. Speak aloud with authority in your voice: "Spirit of fear, go now in the name of Jesus. Holy Spirit, fill my heart in the name of Jesus." Repeat this until fear leaves. Say this for anxiety, depression, and anger. Say it to anything that is taking control of your life.

When Peter was in the boat, he walked on water if he kept his eyes on Jesus. He began to sink when he looked around and saw all the wind and waves. He did not trust Jesus for a minute. He thought his circumstances were bigger than Jesus. Trust all your problems to Jesus, and He will allow you to walk on the storms of your life and stand next to Him on the water. *Matthew 17:20* says, "He said to them, because of your little faith. For truly, I say to you, if you have faith as small as a mustard seed, you will say to this mountain, move from here to there, and it will move, and nothing will be impossible for you."

When you finally ask Jesus to save you from this life, it is as if He is tapping you out when you are being pulverized. He says, "What took you so long to look up?" But when He does save you, you begin to feel disgusted for taking a beating for so long without looking up.

When someone says they are saved, that is what it means. They are saved in every sense of the word. Their soul is saved from torment and an eternity of fire. Their life in the here and now is transformed in unimaginable ways. It is such a precious gift. The devil wants to ensure you never accept or receive it. He does not want you to find the refuge of Jesus. He is a safe place to hide from this cruel world. That is why I am yelling it from the mountaintops. I want everyone to know they can have this refuge and power. I want everyone to know they can have peace, patience, joy, love, and everything the Holy Spirit brings once they trust Jesus to be their Lord and Savior.

Speak His Name

When someone mentions the name of Jesus to an unbeliever, they are disgusted and want that person to stop talking about Him. They say that person is a religious fanatic or a Jesus freak. That is because demons whisper lies into their ears and will not allow them to hear the truth because all the evil plots against their life would become null and void. The most beautiful name I have ever been called is Jesus Freak! It is the best-kept secret of this life. I want to shout it from the mountain tops. I praise Jesus every day for plucking me out of the life I was living.

I was speaking to a friend about Jesus, and she was extremely uncomfortable. I said, "You must admit I was the drunk girl at the party for 35 years. Once I was saved, Jesus laid that down for me." She said, "I do have to admit you did just lay that down." I said, "I did not do anything. Jesus did it. You did not once hear me talk about recovering from alcohol addiction. You did not once say I was trying to quit drinking. You did not once hear me say I received a chip for staying sober for a week or a month. He changed my heart's desires. He told me I did not have to live like that anymore."

Alcohol abuse has brought me nothing but pain and suffering. I did things that I would not have usually done. I said things I would not have typically said. I do not miss waking up in the mornings after a night of drunkenness to a call where someone asked if I remember doing or saying something last night. Alcohol destroys your life while making you think it is a fun time. It made a fool of me and then destroyed my life in the process.

The friend I was speaking to also knows I love to eat as much as she does. So, I pointed out how I could go for two weeks without eating through no doing of my own. I sat at tables in nice restaurants while she ate, and I had nothing.

I am a walking, talking testimony to what Jesus can do in your life. He can make everyone's life better if they trust Him. All you must do is pretend your life is an airplane. Now jump out and use Jesus as your parachute! Your life will change for the good. You will watch all the negative things in your life fall at your feet. He will make you a new, better person. Your life will become so much sweeter. It may not happen in a day, week, or month, but look at your life in a year. You will see that it looks vastly different than it did before you accepted Jesus as your Lord and Savior.

Why Read the Bible

I wondered why I often heard prophetic "downloads" from God, but my saved husband never spoke of any word he received. I realized I read the Bible and spoke to the Holy Spirit daily. Whether you understand the Bible or not, the Holy Spirit speaks to you while you read it! He speaks to you supernaturally. It is the only book where the author will sit with you while you read it.

In other parts of the world, people are dying because they secretly read the Bible. We have one in every home; many do not even open them. They are just decorations collecting dust to make everyone think you are a good person who reads the Bible. I know because I have carried a Bible in my pretend Christian life to give that illusion that I was a real Christian.

Reading the Bible will do more for your life than counseling, medication, or therapy. If you go to therapy or think you need therapy, I implore you to read the Bible four times a week for just fifteen minutes each time. See what happens. What can it hurt? Nothing. But what can it possibly help?

When you read the Bible, you suddenly become wise. You understand concepts that were previously a mystery. You speak truths into your own life and those around you. You become a walking, talking testimony of what God can do in your life. People seek the help of therapists and doctors for so many ailments. If they only knew reading their Bible would bring so much to their lives. Many problems life brings are remedied by picking up a Bible and reading. Read it four times a week, and you will see transformations in your life.

Reading the Bible gives you tools to help you live peacefully and confidently. It also affords you wisdom to use in everyday situations. Many seek therapists and doctors to solve their problems. If they only knew, picking up their dust-covered Bibles would solve many of the problems of this life. The devil wants to ensure no one knows this information because he wants to keep us all living in bondage. The Bible is a bondage breaker!

The Center for Biblical Engagement did a study in 2009 that investigated statistics of people who read the Bible. The statistics are from people who read the Bible at least four times a week. The study showed the following:

Getting Drunk ↓ 57%
Sex Outside Marriage ↓ 68%
Loneliness ↓ 30%
Suicidal Thoughts ↓ 32%
Feeling Ashamed ↓ 32%
Fear and Anxiety ↓ 14%
Lashing Out in Anger ↓ 31%
Gossiping ↓ 28%
Lying ↓ 28%
Pornography ↓ 61%

Some things increase once you start your journey of reading the Bible.

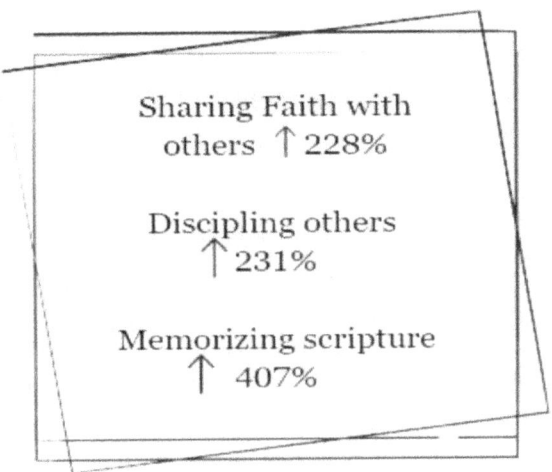

Sharing Faith with others ↑ 228%

Discipling others ↑ 231%

Memorizing scripture ↑ 407%

Before reading the Bible from cover to cover, pray to God and ask for understanding of the word. Remember to always add "in Jesus' name" to the end of all prayers.

These "downloads," so to speak, are just concepts you suddenly know are true. You cannot explain how you know; you just know in your heart. It is different than suspecting something to be true. It is knowing the truth. This started happening to me a few months after my salvation.

Looking back, I realize it started when I began reading the Bible.

People go to church trusting their pastor to tell them what is in the Bible and explain the concepts. You should not put your trust in a fleshly person. Even the most well-intentioned people can accidentally lead you astray. You must read the words yourself. You may say, "But I don't understand what I'm reading." Just keep reading. I promise it will be worth it! Also, do not think, "I hate reading" or "I'm not smart enough to read and understand it." It is more than reading the words. It is alive! God is in the book. That is His word, and He is alive there. It sounds ridiculous and hard to grasp, but it is the truth. Salvation is a life-changing experience, to say the least, but reading the Bible is the battery of the new gift you have received! God rewards faithfulness, and reading His word shows faithfulness.

When you hear someone say, "The Bible has been manipulated," say to them the Holy Spirit speaks to my heart when I read, and no man can manipulate that. Wisdom just comes. For instance, it was put on my heart, and then I read in Genesis that there is a firmament. On the other side of that firmament or glass dome is water. Waters of heaven. This is what makes the sky blue. Have you ever seen a whole rainbow? It is an arch because it is the shape of that dome. Genesis speaks of a firmament separating the earth's waters from the waters of heaven. Read the *Book of Enoch* for interesting concepts on the planet.

A Supernatural Understanding

The first download I received after salvation was that demons and angels are in a constant battle for our souls. They are around us all day, every day. They watch us and every move we make. They monitor our body language. They monitor every spoken word we say. Because they know we will speak aloud what is in our hearts. Because demons cannot hear our thoughts, only what we speak and our body language. They cannot see our hearts; only God can see what is truly in our hearts. So, if they can hear our words, see our actions, and read our body language, they think they know what is in our hearts. They can see things we watch for entertainment. They can hear what we listen to and see the places we go. They use this information to lead us astray and further into sin. They gain control over a person through sin.

Every sin you commit opens a door for a demon to enter your life. Every "yes" you give a demon gives him increased control over you. You give a demon a "yes" through willful sin, witchcraft (tarot cards, opening the third eye, psychics, Ouija boards, necromancy- speaking to the dead), fears, unforgiveness, false religions, ungodly soul ties, abuse, trauma, cursed objects, and cursed buildings. I will speak further on this later. Demons are jealous of humans and seek to destroy us at any given opportunity. They want nothing more than to destroy our lives and send us to hell for eternity. When Satan realized how much God loved us, he grew very jealous. He knew he would never see the kingdom of heaven again and wanted to ensure no human was ever granted access. *John* says, "The thief comes only to steal, kill, and destroy. I came that they may have life and have it abundantly." The enemy will whisper thoughts into your ear. These thoughts are lies meant to lead you in the wrong direction. Take every thought captive. *2 Corinthians 10:5* says, "We destroy every proud obstacle that keeps people from knowing God. We capture their rebellious thoughts and teach them to obey Christ." If any thought that seems strange comes into your mind, analyze it. Demons cannot confess that Jesus is Lord or that He died and rose again for our sins. So, ask that simple fact aloud after a strange thought comes to mind.

The more someone sins, the less protection they have from heaven. Willful sin is how demons receive invitations to come into your life. People are quick to blame God for the sorrow in their lives yet refuse to look at their actions that may have caused an attack. I understand, however, that most people do not know they are being attacked due to sin.

The devil cannot wait for a saved Christian to sin. A believer sinning is like filet mignon for the demons! He prowls around like a lion, waiting to devour anyone he can. He hates saved Christians because they are helping to build the kingdom of heaven. He loses souls when saved Christians share their testimonies and the good news about Jesus with others. Jesus gave believers the gift of losing the will to sin. When you deliberately go against that gift and sin anyway, you give demons the right to attack you. You deliberately lower your hedge of protection from heaven. Sin causes death, so decrease your demons and decrease your odds of dying.

The devil lives in all things that are of the flesh. The vilest sins are sins of the flesh. Murder, drinking, doing drugs, immoral sex acts, lying, and overeating are all done from the flesh. The seven deadly sins are pride, envy, wrath, gluttony, lust, sloth, and greed. Do you see that all of these relate to the flesh in one way or another? The enemy attacks everything to do with the flesh. Fleshly sins are man's greatest downfall. Every sin is committed with the flesh. Flesh can become diseased and die. God never intended for us to become diseased and die. But the first sin, disobeying God, came with disease and death.

Life is a daily spiritual battle. You start each day with a heavenly hedge of protection that is decreased each time you sin. But, as sin creeps in, your hedge of protection gets smaller and smaller. Sin usually starts with a lie a demon whispers in your ear. Each time you sin, that protection goes lower and lower. This is why the Bible says, "The wages of sin is death, but the gift of God is eternal life in Christ Jesus our Lord" (*Romans 6:23*). This means that when you sin, you step one foot closer to death. Both physical death and spiritual death. The enemy wins the more you sin. Death is sin when it is fully grown.

Demons want to cause chaos and destruction in everyone's life. The ways to keep their attacks at bay are to decrease sin, increase praise, and increase worship of the God of heaven. Worry and fear should be replaced with peace, joy, and faith. Also, joy and peace are not decisions you make once you are saved. It just happens. Once Jesus saves you, your whole life changes. It is no doing of your own. He steps in and helps you live your life in a way that helps you cope with living on this earth. All glory goes to Him.

I never understood these things I would hear at church, but now they all make complete sense. The songs I have sung at church all speak to my heart now. Also, you must give a consistent "yes" to Jesus for Him to step in and change your life. I spoke of giving a "yes" to the demons and what it does for your life. The opposite is true once you give a "yes" to Jesus. A "yes" to Jesus is life. The life you are living in the here and now and life after the death of the flesh.

A "yes" to demons equals death. Death in the here and now and death after the flesh dies. It is so easy and hard at the same time. It is a gift the Father gives us. All we must do is accept it. Again, it is the best-kept secret of this life. It is a secret because the demons will not allow us to hear the truth. They try to keep us constantly distracted and entertained.

Loving our neighbor (meaning any other person) and forgiveness are essential parts of this life. But the most important commandment is to "love the Lord your God with all your heart and with all your soul, and with all your mind" (*Matthew 22:37*). Once you surrender your life to Him, you will see why you should love Him so much! If you seek the kingdom of heaven before all decisions, your crooked path will be made straight. *Proverbs 3:6* says, "Seek His will in all you do, and He will show you which path to take."

I worked on this book for about a year when I decided to go to a women's prayer group at The Refuge. Fifty to sixty women were already familiar with everything I was uncovering! God guided me to that group to let me know I was not alone. Before meeting those ladies, no one I knew talked about spiritual warfare and fighting demons. If I mentioned it to anyone, I would receive the strangest looks. Steel sharpens steel, and this group sharpens my sword. They were influential in shaping this book. We would have classes on spiritual warfare and casting out demons. It was nice to speak to other people who knew the truths I was discovering through talking to God and extensive research.

God is building His army of spiritual warriors! We can all benefit from learning the concepts of spiritual warfare in today's world. We can all learn from each other. Let's all learn to be bold and fight evil together! Let's learn to stop hating each other and instead hate the devil. He is the one attacking us. I pray we stop attacking each other and all stand shoulder-to-shoulder against the devil! I also pray we can all step into our authority through Jesus. Because we are weak, BUT HE IS STRONG!

Chapter 3

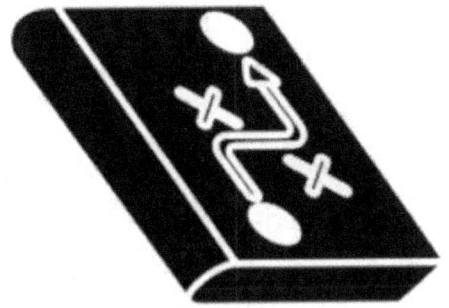

The Enemy's Playbook

When football teams practice, it sometimes includes watching videos of the opposing team playing the game This is to determine any weaknesses of the enemy. Sometimes, people say not to pay attention to the enemy, but I want to know my opponent and how they operate. Most importantly, how and why they attack me! The devil would love for us to look the other way and keep taking a beating. "Move along, nothing to see here." In a war, you want to know how the enemy attacks you and their weaknesses. We cannot fight because we are uneducated about the demons. They know that and laugh at us because we are uninformed about how they attack and why. This book helps give you the tools to fight back. We are all fighting against an unseen enemy. Put all the weapons discussed in this book to work and watch your life transform into something you could have never imagined!

Satan hates us because we are the reason he was punished. When Adam and Eve transgressed, he became a serpent to eat dust. He has been attacking humanity since that day. He is also angry that humans were promised the kingdom of heaven where he once lived. He is trying to ensure that all descendants of Adam will not inherit the kingdom of heaven.

Are demons the one-third of angels that fell from heaven with Lucifer? Are they the disembodied spirits of the Nephilim that perished in the great flood? For those who do not know, the Nephilim are a group of beings that came about through disobedience to God. They result from the angels coming to earth, finding earthly wives, and producing offspring. These offspring were large and evil. They are the giants we have heard about in fairy tales. They eventually became man-eaters because their appetites were insatiable. When God flooded the earth; it was to do away with these evil giants destroying His creation.

No matter where these demons came from, the fact is they hate humans and want nothing more than to see their destruction after causing pain and suffering in their lives. They are jealous of humans because we are the apple of God's eye. They wish they lived in heaven instead of hell. Hell is constant sorrow, pain, and suffering. It reeks of sulfur or rotten eggs.

When a demon is near, it sometimes emits a smell. You may smell sulfur or rotten eggs, cigarette smoke, regular smoke, decay, feces, burning hair, and skunks. Do they smell this way because they are from hell, and this is what hell smells like? Possibly. The smell comes when nothing in the environment has caused it.

I was in my basement after getting saved. I smelled rotten eggs, but there was nowhere the smell would have come from. I grinned and said, "You obviously do not know who I am. I am a child of God, bought and paid for at the foot the cross. I command you to leave my house right now in the name of Jesus!" The smell was gone in an instant. Another instance was when there was an egg smell in my house for two days. My husband called a plumber because he thought it was sewage. I was in bed and remembered that demons smell like rotten eggs. I got up, anointed my house with oil, and commanded all evil to leave in the name of Jesus. The smell was gone! My husband got home and said, "The egg smell is gone." I said, "It was a demon." I have known about this warfare since early in my walk with Christ, but I do not hear people talking about it that much, even in church. Many Christians fear demons and think we should not talk about them because it will make them come. The truth is they are here, and we, as saved Christians, have power over them, but only by speaking the name of Jesus. I will say again that the devil has made Christians deaf, dumb, and fearful of the concept of spiritual warfare. However, through this book and others like it, we will take our power back from the enemy.

Demons can be cast out more efficiently by calling them by name. While demons have names they can also be called out by the destruction they cause. For instance, demons causing pain, demons causing cancer, and demons causing poverty can all be called out. Some demons come with a specific job and come in through something you agreed to or your ancestors agreed to and never dealt with. God Almighty is a sovereign God, but the devil is not. The devil only comes when he is given an invitation. God is everywhere. We invite the devil in and begin to wonder how our lives became so chaotic and destroyed.

Demons are called out by what they cause. Call them out by name when commanding them to leave. Be specific. If it is a disease, speak the name of the disease aloud. If it is any type of addiction, say aloud whatever the addiction is. If it is a mental disorder, speak the disorder aloud. Speak with authority using the name of Jesus. They will submit to that name. Names are important in the spirit realm. Speaking to them aloud is powerful. Demons have names but respond to the chaos and turmoil that they are assigned to carry out. Speak their name. I have included a list of names demons go by. If you are experiencing a problem not on this list, speak the problem aloud.

Demon of:

Poverty	Incest
Incest	Deception
Anger	Gluttony
Fear	Pride
Homosexuality	Greed
Depression	Sloth
Anxiety	Laziness
Addiction	Gambling
Mental Illness	Diseases
Muteness	Pedophilia
Lust	Ungratefulness
Envy	Death

A demon first attacks you by whispering a thought into your mind. It is usually something vile. The demon assesses you to see if you will act on such thoughts. If you do not take these thoughts captive, they will increasingly litter your brain. If a thought comes into your mind that does not sound like something from you, do not ignore it. Stop and say, "I know that thought was not my own, and I rebuke it and command it to leave this instance in the name of Jesus!" The demons will begin to know you will not fall for their secret and destructive tactics. Thoughts may come to your mind that degrade others, thoughts that have you hurting others, thoughts of sexual immorality, suicide, self-loathing, and any evil thought. God did not make us evil beings. The only evil in this world comes from the devil and his evil henchmen, demons. After you tell the thought to leave, praise and worship, quote scripture, and speak peace over your life. Remember, these demons know your body language and facial expressions. Many of these demons have been with you since you were formed in your mother's womb. It is easy for them to make you believe a terrible thought is from you and not them. They are masters of legal entries and know you do not have a clue. They use this to their advantage. A step in the right direction is just reading this book. God wants us to ask questions and not mindlessly follow, but demons want us to follow and obey them without questioning anything. The devil is a liar.

Witchcraft

Do you understand that the devil counterfeits everything God Almighty does? Witchcraft is the counterfeit of Christianity. When people put their faith in anything other than the trinity of God Almighty, Jesus, and the Holy Spirit, they are practicing witchcraft. It is the religion of the devil. I believe many people practicing witchcraft are not aware of this fact. When Christians trust Jesus to save them, they are granted the power of the Holy Spirit. Witches counterfeit this power through the evil power of demons. I dabbled in witchcraft and Wicca when I was in my twenties. I believed in tarot cards and would read tarot cards for others. I would seek advice from psychics, believed in crystals for protection/healing, and I would experiment with simple spells. I had no idea what I was doing. I had no clue what I was inviting into my life. I have prayed for forgiveness and thanked God when those demons fled from me.

Everything witches do is a fake replica of Christians. They will sacrifice animals for their blood. Christians simply claim the blood of Jesus. That is why they say there is power in the blood. Christians have prayers and speak spiritual warfare to the demons in their lives. Witches have spells and incantations that require supplies. Witches believe in crystals, burning sage, and spells for protection, healing, and power. Christians put their faith in the Holy Spirit. When a witch seeks power, it comes from demons. It is a beacon in the spirit realm when you put your faith in anything other than Jesus. It opens a door to demons and invites them in to destroy your life.

You may say, "Sage is just an herb. Why is it bad to burn it?" or "Crystals are from the earth. Didn't God make the earth?" When you put your faith in anything you believe will bring you protection, healing, or power or let you know your future (divination), you turn your back on the Holy Spirit. You are putting your faith in a false idol to provide you with things only God Almighty can provide with no strings attached. When you trust in a false idol, the devil, he will charge you a steep price. If it is not from God Almighty, it is from the devil. Remember the price Adam and Eve paid for trusting the devil? They cursed all of humanity! Put your faith for healing, protection, and peace, and trust your future in the hands of the God of heaven only. He will take you places you have never dreamed of.

You may hear me say occult and witchcraft. I was once confused about the differences between these two concepts. Occult means anything done in secret. All secret societies are evil. Anything that is of God is never held in secret. Witchcraft goes hand in hand with the occult, as it is usually done in secret. Witches work through spells, incantations, potions, sorcery, and supernatural means to influence or predict future events.

Other examples of occult practices are Freemasonry and Satanism. These two groups meet in secret. Freemasons deceive their members into believing they are "spiritual" and believe in a "higher power." That higher power is Satan. They do not disclose this truth to their lower-level members, but some research can prove it. Before disclosing this fact, they want their members to be involved and well-engaged in the program.

These things are cleverly disguised as witchcraft. I bet you didn't know some of them:

Horoscope	Halloween
Yoga	Superstition
Acupuncture	Ouija Board
Palm Reading	Fenshui
Dreamcatchers	Reincarnation
Tarot Cards	Rosary Beads
Astrology	Fortune Cookies
Hypnotism	Numerology
Kundalini	Psychics
Chakras	Spirit Guides

Please do not be deceived!

The Holy Spirit has power over demons. Christians must realize they are much more powerful than witches. Witches do not fear Christians because most of them aren't taught to understand this fact. Everyone sees Christians as weak and passive. While they are meek, at peace, and exude self-control, they have much more power than they realize. I pray this book will help Christians claim the power of the Holy Spirit in Jesus' name!

Monitoring Spirits

Have you ever had a friend or acquaintance who was only interested in learning about your life? These people are not interested in helping you when you need it. They are there to interview you and discover what is happening in your life. These people are possibly working under the influence of a monitoring spirit. Those people are not necessarily evil. They do not know they are being influenced by darkness. Remember, demons cannot hear your thoughts. The spirit plans to get you to talk about what is on your mind. Once they get this information from you, they will take it back to other powers within the hierarchy of the kingdom of darkness. Their only intention is to make you stumble.

Have you ever noticed that when you tell others about your plan, it seems to fall apart? It is because when the devil knows your plan, he deliberately tries to trip you up. He will give you signs and whisper ideas in your ear that will send you down the wrong path. The best way to bring your hopes and dreams to fruition is to keep your plans to yourself! Stay tight-lipped and hold your cards close to your chest.

Monitoring spirits may be trying to oppress you if you have experienced any of the following problems: You feel constantly watched. You may also feel a negative or ominous presence nearby that is watching. Also, if you experience increased intrusiveness from others, do people seem to be exceptionally nosey about your affairs? Another way to know is realizing that you get very close to a goal only to see it fall apart.

Another way to know you are a victim of a monitoring spirit is having constant nightmares. The nightmare will include you being followed, harassed, imprisoned, or attacked. The final way to know you may be experiencing a monitoring spirit is false accusations. Are people accusing you of things you are not guilty of? Are people attacking your character? When someone reaches a massive breakthrough for the kingdom of heaven, you may be a victim of character assassination. This is meant to discredit you. If you are speaking the truth, the only way for demons to get people not to believe you is to discredit your words.

Familiar Spirits

A familiar spirit is a deity that has been with you since you were formed in your mother's womb. It is a demon that is an expert on you and your entire bloodline. They have studied you and your ancestors. They were sent with a sinister plot against you and your descendants. When you trust a psychic or medium, that person talks to the demon that has studied your bloodline. You are not talking to your aunt or uncle who has passed. You are getting information from the demon sent on assignment to destroy all your lives. They can tell you past events that have happened, current events that are happening and lies meant to send you down the wrong path. They cannot prophesy. They do not know what the future holds. Only God Almighty knows the future. If you have put your trust and belief into a psychic, I implore you to seek deliverance. Break all the deals you made with the devil by trusting his lies.

Music

Songs are another way to invite the enemy into your life. Lucifer was the angel controlling music before he was cast out of heaven. He is described in the Bible as the worship director. He understands the power of music and what comes out of people's mouths as a song. All secular music (everyday music you hear on the radio) has everyone singing aloud curses into their own lives. Think of most songs you may hear played on the radio. Words spoken with your mouth are powerful. When they sing aloud, the words invite those things into our lives. It gives demons legal rights to manifest things in your life. Raising your hands while singing the words aloud invites evil when you are at a concert. Raising your hands is a sign of surrender. When we do it at church, it means we surrender to the most high God. Who are you surrendering to at a concert? Not the God of Abraham, Isaac, and Jacob.

There was a concert last year that was used as a satanic ritual to kill and harvest souls for hell. The enemy is not hiding anymore and is doing things in plain sight. People attending concerts should be very aware of any satanic ritual that may be taking place on stage. When they attend, they are a part of that ritual— singing songs that may be a part of it. Using your tongue to sing aloud is enormously powerful. These singers have all the power of agreement with the crowd. Everyone singing in unison as an army of tongues for destruction!

Part of spiritual warfare includes songs that praise Jesus. This weapon is used against the enemy like a sword used in battle. We battle not against flesh and blood. *Ephesians 6:12*: "For our struggle is not against flesh and blood, but against the rulers, against the authorities, against the powers of this dark world, and against the spiritual forces of evil in the heavenly realms." When people sing praise and worship in unison, it is like an army firing missiles at the enemy!

Pictures

Do you have any pictures of yourself or your kids on social media? Witches send curses and attack people through their pictures. If you can see your eyes in the picture, they can use your picture in a ritual where they burn it or wrap it in different elements to curse you. While I do not fear witches, I deliberately left my picture off this book for this reason. I do not want to give them an easy avenue to attack me. Even when it is not a witch putting a curse on you, please do not underestimate the power of envy and jealousy in anyone. Everyone puts only the wonderful parts of their life on social media. This leads to jealousy and causes people to speak word curses over you. Someone who speaks negatively about another person is speaking a curse over that person.

Have you ever seen someone's pictures on social media and felt jealous over something they posted? Have you ever said something unkind when you saw someone's pictures on social media? I imagine someone has said something unkind about your pictures as well. Protect yourself and your family.

Narcissism

Have you ever known someone whom you would consider to be narcissistic? Have you ever known two of them or more? Do you see similarities in the way they behave? It is because the same demons influence them. That is because they operate under three separate demons working together to make this personality. The spirit of Leviathan is the first one. You may have seen the colossal snake monster in the sea. Yes, this is the one. This spirit is prideful and brings confusion. This is the person who stirs the pot or twists someone's words. They will then speak these words into someone's ears. This demon can destroy almost anything by bringing confusion, chaos, judgment, and arrogance.

The second spirit working in someone who suffers from narcissism is the evil spirit of Jezebel. The Jezebel spirit is more subtle than the Leviathan spirit. The Jezebel spirit comes with cunning, seduction, and deception. Also, the Jezebel spirit can operate in a man or a woman. However, the seductive manner of the Jezebel spirit will lure a married man into adultery. The devil wants to destroy any covenant made through and by God Almighty. That spirit will then laugh at what it caused. The Jezebel spirit is exceptionally charming to get what it wants.

The spirit of Ahab is the third spirit that operates in a narcissistic person. The spirit of Ahab refuses to take responsibility and stand for what is true. Do you know any narcissistic people who will never own up to anything they cause? They cannot fathom being at fault for anything wrong that happens. They would also think, "How dare you suggest I am at fault." They are the people for whom the word "gaslighting" was coined. That is the spirit of Leviathan rearing its ugly head. They try to make you believe something did not happen the way you remember it, thus instilling confusion in the situation. They will then tell a lie to cover up an essential aspect of the situation or change the details of the situation. Lastly, they will tell you it is all your fault, and they are the victims in the whole situation.

Boom! Narcissism is broken down by the demons at work in those people. If you know two narcissistic people, you can see their similarities. As I said, it is because the same demons work in them. If you are a victim of a narcissistic person, research information regarding dealing with these spirits. I could write a whole book on this subject! I have been a victim of a few narcissistic people in my life.

Distractions

Demons want to distract and entertain you so you will never see what they are doing. My TV used to stay on for twenty-four hours a day. Now, I hardly watch TV. I do not listen to secular music anymore. Singing music is a weapon. The songs you sing are speaking curses or blessings into your life and the lives of your descendants. Movies are meant to distract us. Sports are also meant to distract us. Anything we consider a pastime or entertainment distracts us from developing a closer relationship with God, thus increasing the number of attacks we sustain from the enemy. Reread that. Have you ever stayed up until 2 watching TV, but you are sleepy as soon as you want to read your Bible?

I bet you think I lead a boring life. I want to insert a laughing emoji here. But, on the contrary, I have never felt so alive! I used to exist merely. I used to spend my days wondering where I could go for entertainment and get drunk while I was there. Now, I spend my days looking for the good I can do for someone I do not know and can never repay me for what I have done for them. I know; I still have not made my life sound great. That is the beauty of Jesus. He makes you love your life just as it is. I have always heard, "The best things in this life are free." They are! Demons are the ones who try to steal your joy, but Jesus keeps filling your cup. Everything in this world is meant to distract us from realizing who we are: children of the Almighty God. We are so loved and powerful through Jesus. It's incredible. We have all this power and have no clue. All we must do is believe!

Depression and Anxiety

In my pretend Christian life, I was on anti-anxiety meds and antidepressant meds. I took those medications for twenty-five years! When I trusted Jesus, anxiety and depression left along with the alcohol addiction. My mind had been riddled with fear and sadness for many years. I wanted to give up and die when I finally looked up to the heavens. I felt everyone else had it all together, but not me. I was struggling to be the kind of person this world considered worthwhile. I now realize I have nothing to prove to anyone on this planet any longer. What a liberating feeling! I have been set free from the bondage of this world. Jesus came because we all need freedom.

Jesus came to set the captives free and I thank Him every day that I was one of those captives He freed.

I know anxiety and depression are crippling and touch every aspect of your life. Surprise! They are demons. They can be rebuked, bound up, and cast out. Just say the words over them. Command them to leave in the name of Jesus. Tell them you revoke any invitation you gave them to come into your life. Wake up each morning and plead the blood of Jesus aloud over your life and watch them leave. It is that simple.

Abortion

I want to shout this one from the mountaintops because the devil has deceived many people. The act of having an abortion makes a blood contract with Satan. It is making a deal with the devil. Whatever the reason you have for seeking an abortion will then be the way Satan will destroy your life. Let me elaborate. Say you had the baby aborted because you could not afford to have it. The blood contract would mean that you would live in poverty after killing the baby. Everything you have in this life will be a struggle to obtain and will always fall through your hands like sand in the wind. I promise you that abortion is strictly the devil's ground. The devil will not give you anything without taking much more than he gave you.

Some think it is a question of a woman's body. This is a highly simplistic way of thinking. Anyone who has ever given any true thought to abortion knows it is murder. It is sacrificing your baby to Moloch. The little "g" god or demon of child sacrifice. It is not an issue that is simply a question of someone's body. If they have an abortion, they should be informed that the baby is being sacrificed to a demon. They should also see the contract they are coming into agreement with. Satan is a liar, and he loves making contracts with people. When they sign the paperwork for the abortion, they agree to the contract.

Am I telling you this because I am a goody-two-shoes who wants to sit on my high throne and judge everyone? Absolutely not. I once believed wholeheartedly in abortion. I had an abortion myself when I was young and did not know what I was doing. I have often fallen to my knees and on my face, asking for forgiveness for that sin. I know Jesus forgave me. I pray I see that child in heaven. I am just here to warn others of what these horrible demons do to our lives. As I said, I am fully awake and have a duty to warn others. I know abortion is a touchy subject that is politically charged. However, if you do not believe what I have said, I implore you to investigate and prove me wrong.

When angry at others, we must hate the evil spirit behind their actions, not the person. Satan will lose, and humanity will win if we all abide by this. Let's all love each other and hate the devil.

Fame and Fortune

Satan lures people in with the promise of fame, fortune, and power. While that sounds enticing, he will not give it to you for free. The devil will take much more from you than he ever gave you. This world is temporary. The rewards you receive from following Satan will send you down a path to hell. This life is a blink of an eye compared to eternity. Satan will fill you with promises for this life but will give you an eternity of self-loathing, pain, sorrow, and burning.

Performers and actors have in their contracts that they are not to speak the name of Jesus while they are on set in the studio. This should tell you everything you need to know about fame and fortune. You should see clearly who runs that industry.

Since God gives only good and the devil gives only bad, imagine a place where the God of heaven does not exist. You experience good and evil in this life. If you count on Satan, you will only experience the bad for eternity. When your spirit goes to heaven, you will only experience good because demons are not there. Satan has those who follow him believing he cares about them. If they only knew he was using them to conduct his nefarious plot on all of humanity. He does not care about them. They are disposable to him.

God Almighty watches and is very sorrowful because some people choose to follow Satan. He says, "My people will perish for lack of knowledge" in *Hosea 4:6*. When people very mindlessly follow Satan, they perish when their flesh dies. If you keep your eyes on the God of heaven, he will come near you. Resist the devil, and he will flee from you (*James 4:7*).

Spirit Guides

Spirit Guides are another way the enemy gets you to invite him in. When you communicate with a spirit guide, it is not an angel with your best interest at heart. A spirit guide is a demon. That is why we are warned not to speak to the angels of the spirit realm. This permits the demons to enter your life. They will then have your permission to destroy your life. I have heard people say their spirit guide is the disembodied spirit of their ancestors, helping to guide them through this life. This is incorrect. We only talk to God almighty, Jesus, or the Holy Spirit. Accessing the spirit realm is dangerous without the Holy Spirit. When you do, the demons have permission to attack you. This is part of their legal rights. As I said before, demons are experts in legal rights and will take advantage of everything you do that invites them to destroy you. People may argue that the spirit was kind to them. Demons will be kind and helpful to gain your trust. After they have gained your trust, they will slowly demolish and dismantle your life piece by piece.

Pagan Holidays

The devil is going to rear his ugly head on this one. *Jeremiah 10:2-5* says, "This is what the Lord says: Do not act like the other nations, who try to read their future in the stars. Do not fear their predictions, even though other nations are terrified by them. Their ways are futile and foolish. They cut down a tree, and a craftsman carves an idol. They decorate it with gold and silver and then fasten it securely with hammer and nails, so it won't fall over. Their gods are like helpless scarecrows in a cucumber field! They cannot speak and need to be carried because they cannot walk. Do not be afraid of such gods, for they can neither harm you nor do you any good." Does that sound like a Christmas tree?

Christmas and Easter are holidays designed to have Christians celebrate the wrong things. The Bible never mentions the date of Jesus' birth. "Shepherds were in their fields keeping watch on their flocks at night" (Luke 2:8). Shepherds were only in their fields at night during one time of the year: spring. Lambs are born in the spring, and the shepherds watch over the sheep through the night to help them give birth. '

It is interesting how Jesus is the sacrificial lamb of the world and was born when the other lambs were born. Before Jesus died for our sins, people had to sacrifice animals to ask for forgiveness for their sins. Once Jesus was crucified, he was the ultimate sacrifice for the whole world's sins. However, you must accept the gift of this sacrifice. We are not born forgiven for our sins. We must surrender to Jesus to be forgiven.

Christmas has us all celebrating two demons. Saturnalia was a time of year to celebrate the little "g" god or demon called Saturn. Saturnalia is where we get Christmas trees, wreaths, lights, and mistletoes and exchange gifts. This was a time of year when people would participate in getting drunk, getting together, feasting, and doing things you would not normally do and call it normal.

The second little "g" god or demon was Odin. Odin went on a yearly hunt called the Wild Hunt. He rode across the sky looking for souls. Anyone unable to hide from him was snatched. If you were in Odin's good graces, you would receive gifts. If not, you would be killed. He has "elves" who make the gifts he distributes.

Santa Claus also flies across the sky. Santa Claus comes with the tagline "Believe." Young people look to adults they trust who tell them Santa is real. Christmas has us believing in Santa Claus only to find out he is fake. This sets us up to not trust or believe in Jesus. Once people realize Santa is not real, they are leery of believing in

Anyone else from the people they trust, for example, Jesus.

The letters of Santa are Satan, as in Satan's claws. Jesus' gifts are much more than Santa Claus ever imagined. I know it is a tough pill to swallow because it is what we have been taught our whole lives. I remind you again that Satan is a liar. He will do anything to have people worship him instead of the God of heaven.

Easter has turned the resurrection of Christ into bunnies and eggs. Neither of these has to do with Christ. They are symbols of the god of fertility. Easter is about a sex orgy where even virgins were made to lay in the temple of Ishtar and have sex with anyone who entered. The children would be born near the end of December, or Christmas, and sacrificed to Ishtar that Easter. They would take eggs and dip them in the blood of that baby to complete the ritual. This is a Pagan holiday where the conception, yes, the conception, of Tammuz is celebrated. He was the offspring of Ishtar and Nimrod. Nimrod was the son of Ishtar. Tammuz was their child! Nimrod was also the enemy of God, who built Babylon. Easter is also a time when people who worship Satan have multiple sacrifices.

Have you ever asked, "Why is Good Friday the day Jesus was crucified? He was resurrected on Sunday?" Is that two or three days? Hmmm. He was resurrected after three days and three nights. We have always just accepted what we have been told. Ask questions!

Satan tells his followers that Jesus was a sacrifice to him. They kidnap an unsuspecting person and do a ritualistic sacrifice on the cross.

Halloween is obviously to celebrate Satan. Halloween is the biggest night of witchcraft of the entire year. People who worship Satan do rituals and sacrifices and put curses on people. Witches curse the candy that is distributed to give to our children. Satan is thrilled that parents allow their children to celebrate him. Satan wants nothing more than for us to celebrate him and turn our backs on God Almighty. I used to love Halloween. It was one of my favorite times of the year. Not anymore.

We have all been told since childhood to celebrate these holidays. Most people have not questioned the idea. I never questioned these holidays until I was saved and the Holy Spirit gave me many truths. I now consult the Holy Spirit for truth when people tell me something is untrue. So many people are still blind.

Satan depends on the ignorance of people. He depends on the ones who do not know the power of Jesus Christ and the power He has given us. The devil relies on people who do not know. The devil is powerless against the name of Jesus Christ spoken by a saved believer! The Holy Spirit now lives in their heart. The Holy Spirit tramples demons like a giant ocean wave over a child's sandcastle! It is not even a contest. I know that I am going to receive much criticism over this truth. I am including what is put in my heart in this book. When people get uncomfortable around you, it is because the Holy Spirit that lives in you bothers their demons. Demons know when there is light in your heart. They will often whisper something terrible about you in the ear of the person in front of you to get that person to leave your presence. Demons have no power over the light, as darkness cannot exist where there is light.

I have witnessed people staring at me with disgust in public—people to whom I have not spoken a word. They were five feet away, frozen with scowls on their faces. I did not know what to make of it at first, but now I completely understand.

Healthcare and Medication

Another demon I feel led to include is the demon of pharmakeia. Medicine, either over-the-counter or prescription, gives us a laundry list of other health problems when it solves one. This is by design. Medicine is supposed to keep us sick and not heal us. People are so quick to trust what a doctor tells them mindlessly. While talking to a doctor has its place, we should not unquestioningly trust anyone to care for our health. No one cares about your health as much as you do. Doctors are taught through college. The college also develops a curriculum to keep the doctors in the dark. They are not taught anything other than to prescribe medication or recommend surgery. When was the last time you went to see a doctor with a problem and left without a prescription? When the medications are ineffective, they recommend surgery. Have you ever stopped to think about why this is? It is ultimately evil due to the money it generates.

Look up a picture of the Baphomet statue. It has caduceus on its stomach. The caduceus is the two snakes climbing up a rod that symbolizes healthcare. For those who do not know what the Baphomet is, it is a demonic statue that many Satanists worship. Also, have you ever read the oath that doctors must take? It is called the Hippocratic oath. That sounds like "hypocrite", doesn't it? The Hippocratic oath is to "gods" and "goddesses," which are demons. Apollo was not only the "god" of healthcare but was also known to spread plagues among the people to control the masses. There is nothing new under the sun.

The bottom line is that you should never mindlessly listen to anyone who tells you definitively what to do with your health. After being told what to do, research for yourself or always get a second or third opinion.

Homosexuality

I know this is a delicate subject. I want everyone living with homosexual thoughts to realize they can have power over it. Some may think they do not want to get rid of it. But life is so much more complicated than it should be. You would not have to worry about what your friends and family think. You would not have to explain yourself at every turn.

I know that everything that left me when I was truly saved was a demon. That is how I know it is a demon that causes it. I, too, experienced homosexual thoughts until the Holy Spirit came to live in me. All the things that left in me, I now know, were demons. I am genuinely trying to help those who are being oppressed by this demon. I have never shared this information with anyone.

When people tell me they were born this way, I suspect that to be true. This is because of generational or inherited curses. Demons are given the right to attack us in the womb. The devil will stop at nothing to ensure he causes chaos and confusion amongst humanity. He is seeking to stop entire bloodlines.

I have such compassion for those who are still living under the deception of this demon. I have had those thoughts since I was young. They just left when I trusted Jesus. I cannot judge anyone living with homosexuality. I want everyone to know it will leave if you trust Jesus.

This book does not come to condemn people. It was written to help give them the tools to fight these terrible entities that attack in secret. I am trying so hard to let people know this is a devil seeking to destroy them. It illuminates the darkness of what the devil does not want to reveal. Ever since I was saved and changed by no doing of my own, I had to warn people of the hateful things the devil does to them. He tries to make their lives more difficult by speaking lies in their ears. Please trust Jesus and watch all those thoughts go away.

Pedophilia

Satan wants nothing more than to corrupt God's creation. When the children are sexually abused, all the demons of the ungodly soul tie go into that child. The child then starts life with an overwhelmingly enormous number of demons. Sometimes, sexual abuse of children also includes a satanic ritual. These satanic rituals invite demons to take over. Demons will do whatever they can to gain access to someone, even children. The demons influence those who are pedophiles. The adult has control over the children, and the demon has control over the pedophile. It is a win-win for the demon. It is so evident to me how Satan is normalizing all things that help to grow his kingdom. Many people in this society mindlessly follow without stopping to think.

Do you see how all things from Satan are mainstream now? The "yes" these pedophiles give to Satan turns into full-blown sexual abuse of children. The demons sit back and smirk because they think they have won.

Spirit Spouses

Anyone who has ever struggled with relationships may be a victim of a spirit spouse. A spirit spouse will attack you while you sleep. A succubus attacks a male, and an incubus attacks a female. There is also the demon of Lilith. These demons are responsible for what is known as a "wet dream." When these demons are having sex with you while you sleep, they become increasingly jealous of you. They will ensure that no person in the physical world will have a healthy relationship with you. They will work hard to sabotage that relationship. The way to get rid of these demons is to repent for your sins and command them to go in the name of Jesus.

This book is not meant to call anyone out or shame anyone. It was meant to warn people of the unseen enemy we fight daily. We must learn to hate the evil spirit that causes someone to behave like they do. We should not judge or hate the person, as they are victims of that spirit oppressing them. We should all have compassion for each other. Judge and hate the evil spirits not the person they are tormenting!

Sometimes, when people say Christians are judgmental, it is because they do not understand their motivation. I, too, thought Christians were judgmental. They are simply warning others of the dangers of sin. I cannot judge anyone as I was the most despicable person I knew. When you begin to live for Jesus, you do not have to change anything. He will do it for you. Once you believe in Jesus, the veil will be lifted, and you will know the truth. The demons who have been tormenting you since birth will have to leave when the Holy Spirit enters and lives in you. Your name will be written in the Lamb's Book of Life.

Chapter 4

Spiritual Warfare: Engaging the Enemy

Now that I have discussed evil, let's explore how to eliminate it and take back our lives! Please keep reading and discover how to shine a light into the darkness and command it to leave.

Prayer is when we speak to our Father in heaven. Spiritual warfare is engaging the enemy. This is how we fight in the spirit realm. We speak to the enemy and command them what to do and where to go in Jesus' name. This is the power we have, as Christians, that churches do not talk about enough. Spiritual warfare should be explained in every sermon.

When I was first saved, the most significant understanding that came to me was the concept of spiritual warfare. I thought, "I'm in a war that I've known nothing about my whole life!" I was being attacked and just taking it. I now fight back all day, every day. I read every book I can get my hands on about the subject. Not just read them, study them.

My life looks much different than before I found out this information. I was pulled out of that life because I am a strong spiritual warrior for Christ. The demons kept me living that life for so long because they knew who I was and did not want me to find out. You, too, can see those chains of addiction, suicidal thoughts, depression, anxiety, and fear fall at your feet. You can become the person the creator intended you to be. It is fantastic to realize you weren't put here to struggle but with a purpose. Your life will begin to have meaning.

Before we continue, speak this aloud: Demons in and around me, I silence you in the mighty name of Jesus. I block you from whispering in my ears. I command you to leave and allow me to read these words with understanding in the name of Jesus.

You see, demons will hate that you are reading this information. They will do whatever they can to distract you. They will tell you these words are not the truth. You have power, my friend, speaking the name of Jesus, and they do not want you to know. These are the secrets to spiritual warfare.

Many Christians will say, "Do not talk about demons. It will invite them in." Sorry to be the bearer of bad news, but they are already here. You are losing the fight because you do not realize you are in one. We are all in the fight for our existence and have no idea! It is of the utmost importance to understand that ALL things are spiritual before they are physical.

There are always demons and angels in a war around us. A fight for our souls. When you ask Jesus to come into your heart, demons will leave. The Holy Spirit fills your heart, and demons cannot live there anymore. Demons control many aspects of your life and are there to destroy you at every opportunity. Their goal is to send your soul to hell after destroying your life. When you sin, you decrease your hedge of protection from God. Once you are saved, you lose the desire to sin. This increases your hedge of protection. This is why Scripture says that all things work together for the good of those who love God. He protects you from the possession of demons. Demons place a veil over your eyes and deafness over your ears so you cannot see or hear the truth. I know because I lived that way for so long.

Demons can be cast out of someone by a believer in Christ. Demons must submit and flee when cast out in the name of Jesus. When I say, "In the name of Jesus," I mean "Jesus" spoken aloud. The power of the spoken name of Jesus and the Holy Spirit is much more powerful than any witchcraft spell that gets its power from lowly demons. The Holy Spirit is the ruler of all spirits. The reason unbelievers think Christians are _____(insert any word that comes to mind here) is that demons want to make sure people do not discover the truth and step into their power against them. A demon whispered in your ear to tell you how to fill in the blank.

We are all born with a purpose, and it is a purpose for the kingdom of God. Demons want to ensure none of us step into that purpose because their plans will become null and void. Seek God's face, and you will see the truth. God wants us to ask questions. Talk to Him, and He will reveal things to you.

Have you ever wondered why talking about Jesus is so uncomfortable? Demons that live in and around everyone cannot stand to hear His name spoken aloud. Believers will talk about Jesus all day, but to an unbeliever, the name of Jesus is like nails on a chalkboard. I know because I was an unbeliever not long ago. Demons will tell the person listening to get away from that person in any way they can.

Unbelievers cannot and will not be around someone who speaks the name of Jesus. They will do whatever they can to avoid that person. If you are an unbeliever, ask yourself why you feel so uncomfortable when the name of Jesus is mentioned. It is because there is a demon in or around you. That demon knows people who speak that name have faith and power over them. If you eliminate those demons, your life will be so sweet. You will not have an entity following you all day with the sole purpose of destroying your life and sending you to hell. Well, they will still be following you, but you will have spiritual authority over them by speaking the name of Jesus!

Demons are responsible for all terrible things. They can enter your life through your family and ancestors, generationally. They will affect an entire bloodline. Again, I was an alcoholic for 35 years. When I asked Jesus to save me from this life, I stopped drinking without even trying. But, if I continued down that path, my children and grandchildren would be subject to those demons.

I know that demons live in your heart unless you ask Jesus to save you. They flee in an instant. Mental disorders, addiction, anger, sexual immorality, hate, fear, jealousy, homosexuality, adultery, poverty, and anxiety are all caused by demons.

Once you trust Jesus, they leave, and you suddenly have joy in a chaotic situation and peace that does not make sense. You feel love like you have never experienced before being saved.

Everyone who is not saved has demons present and controlling their heart and decisions. When you pray, you develop a relationship with Jesus, and He drives those demons away. He helps you navigate this world. Demons flee at the sound of His name. However, His name must be accompanied by faith for them to flee. It is not just a magic word you say. In the movies, vampires were subject to a cross, but only if the one holding the cross had faith. The demons know if you have faith in Christ or not. It is hard to believe this, but it is the truth. Vampires remind me of demons. You must invite them in; they flee with faith in Jesus and the cross; they live on the blood of humans (like satanic rituals); they run rampant at night; they love the dark and hate the light; they are full of deception; they love sexually immoral acts and destroying the lives of humans.

The devil is the king of lies. He ensures you cannot see or hear the truth when you are not saved. This is why people make fun of Christians or roll their eyes when He is talked about. Demons whisper in their ear that the person talking is a Jesus freak, weird, hokey, or again (fill in the blank)_____.

Recording artists and movie stars have it written in their contracts that they cannot say the name of Jesus. This is because demons tremble and flee at the sound of His name. There is power when His name is spoken with faith. I want to share this information with everyone. I know it will be met with opposition, but I still must share it. When God forgives you for a lot, you are so appreciative that you fall on your face and worship Him with all your heart. You will do whatever He puts on you to do. I cannot help but do things that honor Him. You want to show love to those who do not deserve it. You have compassion for others. You do not judge others because you know it is the demons at work in their life. Hate the unclean spirit, not the person.

When I try to warn others of these truths, it may come off as judgmental, but it is from a place of compassion. I have no room to judge anyone. I was the most wretched person I had known for many years. I know this because I know what was on my mind. When you are the drunk girl at the party for 35 years, you do and say things that you are ashamed of. I am ashamed of things that were on my mind and in my heart. Now, my mind is an open book, and I am not ashamed of one thing I think of. I tell people about the love Jesus has for them because I want others to know what I now know. I wish someone had spoken these words to me many years ago.

I now realize that everyone can have salvation and live this life walking free. One person is not more special than another. God loves us all equally. I was the prodigal son (daughter). He chased me down and never gave up on me. He left the ninety-nine to bring me home. All the angels in heaven rejoiced the day I gave my life to Jesus. Did you know the angels rejoice when anyone gives their life to Jesus? You are saved from eternal damnation.

Reading this book is an excellent start to your journey to seek the face of God. Pray to have the veil removed from your eyes and deafness from your ears so you may see and hear the truth. We are all precious in God's sight. He sends His angels to fight for us. He wants us to leave the dark and come into the light. Darkness cannot exist where there is light. Fear cannot exist where there is faith. It is ultimately your decision to come to Jesus, not anyone else's. That is how God designed it. He did not want to force anyone into anything.

When you do not trust God, demons will overrun you. Demons want to do anything to cause chaos, wreak havoc, and destroy your life. They laugh at you all the while. They revel in the fact that they control you and have power over your life. We unknowingly invite them and give them the keys to our entire lives. They are jealous of us because God loves us so much and cast them out of heaven. The way to get rid of them is to say with your mouth and heart, "Jesus, please save me from this life! I know you died for my sins. I am truly sorry for all the sins I have committed. I forgive anyone who has ever wronged me, just as I want you to forgive me now." He will step in and replace all demons that are living rent-free in your heart. He will replace fear, hatred, jealousy, anger, hopelessness, alcoholism/addiction, self-loathing, anxiety, depression, promiscuity, and any other harmful things that have taken over your life. He will replace it with peace, joy, love, and hope. You will begin to become the person God intended you to be when he formed you in your mother's womb. If you ask Jesus to save you and mean it, sit back and watch your life transform in ways you could have never dreamed of!

A perfect example is the game where you fall backward into someone's arms, filled with trust that they will catch you. When you fall into Jesus' arms and trust Him to save you, he will give you a new life. You will remove your old, nasty, torn clothes, and He will give you a bright white robe. You will walk as a new person. You've tried everything else. Why not try Jesus?

When you wake up each morning, speak aloud: I put on the whole armor of God. I put on my helmet of salvation, my breastplate of righteousness, my sword of the Holy Spirit, my shield of faith, my shoes of peace, and my belt of truth in Jesus' name. Amen.

Each time you speak of a piece of armor, imagine you are putting it on in your mind. Pray in the spirit.

Also, speak aloud:

Father, wash me in the blood of Jesus from the crown of my head to the soles of my feet. Keep me safe from all enemy attacks today, in Jesus' mighty name!

Demons abide by a legal system if you can believe that! They are experts in the legal system they operate under. When we say "yes" to sin, we give them legal rights over our lives. In the court system of heaven, God is the judge. Jesus stepped in and paid the price for the sins we committed, and the Holy Spirit is our counsel or advisor. He is a "light for our path and a lamp for our feet" (*Psalm 119:105*).

Demons will only come in when there is garbage to feed them. Someone addicted to drugs or alcohol invites them in and "feeds" them. Witchcraft, necromancy (trying to communicate with the dead), tarot cards, opening your "third eye," Ouija boards, psychics, horoscopes, burning sage, and casting spells all invite them in. Emotional outbursts such as yelling, crying, raging, and even outbursts of laughter are all food for demons. Think of the Monsters, Inc. movie: Stay calm in all situations, or demons will take over and cause more destruction and chaos. Have you ever felt flustered in a situation, and whatever you are dealing with falls apart? That is due to the demons taking over the situation when you do not look to God Almighty for clarity. The God of heaven brings peace to every situation if we seek Him first. If we choose not to seek Him, the demons can and will take over.

Put on your full armor and engage the enemy straight on. The helmet of salvation keeps the demons from speaking into your ears and trying to deceive you. The breastplate of righteousness is protection when your desire to sin is decreased. The shield of faith is the protection that comes when you put all your trust and confidence in God Almighty. The sword of the Holy Spirit helps you slay the enemy. The sword is sharpened by reading and learning scripture. Your shoes of peace come when the Holy Spirit lives in you. The belt of truth is around your waist, which convicts you to walk in truth all day. Put it on every morning by speaking it aloud. Do not walk in fear any longer. Know who you are. Know your worth. Know your power as a Christian. Step into that power today. Speak aloud, "Come on, Holy Spirit, let's go." Speak quietly and calmly, but walk in the power of the Holy Spirit. Now, let's cast out some demons!

Chapter 5

Cast Out Demons

Before reading any further, please review the warning at the beginning of the book. Now that I have explained how to truly become saved, let me talk about how this is key to casting out demons. Jesus promises we can cast out demons and heal using His name. When a saved person commands demons in the mighty name of Jesus, they must obey.

If you doubt this information is accurate, what if it isn't? What have you lost by doing it? Nothing. But what do you have to gain if it does work? Everything! Trust it and try it for yourself. You will see. Take authority over the darkness.

To cast out demons in someone, you must first resolve the legal reason they have to be there! If it is drugs, they must be willing to give up the addiction. By truly inviting Jesus in, you will automatically want to give up addictions without even trying. Whether occult or witchcraft, they must come with truth in their heart and be willing to lay that down. They must confess their problem and repent fully (ask for forgiveness and truly feel remorseful). Once the person has done this, you can demand the demon to leave in the name of Jesus Christ. Legally, they must leave. Legal reasons for a demon entering:

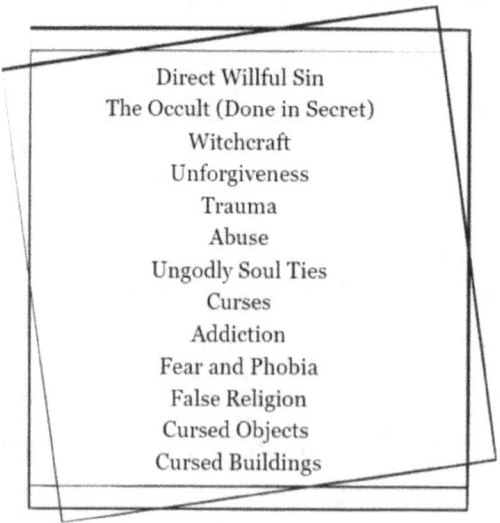

Direct Willful Sin
The Occult (Done in Secret)
Witchcraft
Unforgiveness
Trauma
Abuse
Ungodly Soul Ties
Curses
Addiction
Fear and Phobia
False Religion
Cursed Objects
Cursed Buildings

Renounce any area the demons have entered and cast them out using the name of Jesus. When I say "in the name of Jesus," I mean to say His name aloud.

Telling a little white lie is also a lie. I am trying to live a life free of sin, and I know telling a lie is a sin. When you sin, you are open to demon attacks. Instead of telling a trivial lie, think of a way to tell the truth and omit the information you would tell a "white lie" about.

Direct Willful Sin

When I got saved, I looked up a list of sins to work to decrease them because I suddenly knew this was how the enemy attacked me. We may see this list and think, "God just wants us to be sad, and He takes all the fun out of everything." He is trying to decrease the chances that the enemy will attack us. He gave us the Ten Commandments to decrease the number of attacks we endure. Here is a list of sins, some you may know and some you may not know:

Adultery	Quarrels	Fleshliness
Cheating	Idolatry	Foolishness
Swearing	Jesting	Fornication
Sorcery	Judging	Greed
Swindling	Laying up	Hatred
Unbelief	treasures on earth	Cowardice
Lust	Filthiness	Denying Christ
Malice	Complaining	Desiring praise
Anger	Addiction	of men
Wrath	Drunkenness	Divorce
Murder	Homosexuality	Blasphemy
Pride	Ungratefulness	Boasting
Prostitution	Witchcraft	Brutality
Sensuality	Freemasonry	Being conceited
Hypocrisy	Gambling	Arrogance
Jealousy	Bearing false	Fearfulness
Lying	witness	Strife
Cheating	Coveting	Evil thoughts
Lover of self	Knowing to do	Slander
Envy	good but doing	Unable to
	nothing	forgive

When something terrible happens in our lives, we tend to say, "How could God have allowed this to happen to me?" We blame God when the blame should go to the devil. How do I decrease the number of attacks from the enemy? Decrease the amount of sin in your life and praise Jesus all day. That sounds simple enough, right? If you invite

Jesus to be the Lord of your life, He will make the urge to sin close to nonexistent, thus keeping you safe from enemy attacks.

We get attacked when we are close to reaching a divine breakthrough. The devil will do whatever he can to ensure we never reach the destiny we were put on this earth for. But, if we keep our eyes on God, we will weather the storms Satan puts in our way. God is our refuge and hiding place when the devil attacks us.

A sin is a sin. We all sin. When we sin, it is crucial to ask for forgiveness as soon as we know we have committed it. Demons do not have jurisdiction to attack us for sins for which we have true repentance. *1 Corinthians 6:-10* "Don't you realize that those who do wrong will not inherit the Kingdom of God? Do not fool yourselves. Those who indulge in sexual sin, or who worship idols, or commit adultery, or are male prostitutes, or practice homosexuality, or are thieves, or greedy people, or drunkard, or are abusive, or cheat people-none of these will inherit the Kingdom of God." This is not because God is trying to rule as a tyrant. God loves us and wants us to understand that's how we are attacked. I will say again that Jesus helps you not to sin so that you can decrease your attacks and get closer to the kingdom of heaven.

Say this aloud with authority after reading the warning at the beginning of this book:

Father, reveal to me any sin I allow in my life. I close the door on every demon that came in through sin (speak the specific sin). I command you to leave me now spirit. I renounce_____ Father, I ask you to forgive me for _____. Any demon that thinks they have rights to my life; I command you to loose me now. I bind you up and cast you to the feet of Jesus! I rebuke you and command that you never return in the mighty name of Jesus!

The Occult

The occult is anything done in secret. Darkness is the way the devil moves. His plans are shrouded in secrets and lies. He wants to ensure that no one knows he is attacking them. They are helpless because they are in a war they know nothing about. That is why the devil is the victor over many people's lives.

Three things that are of the occult are Freemasons, Satanists, witches, and any secret society. I know I will get backlash for this truth. I did not make the rules; I just know what they are. If you are angry about what I said, ask yourself, "Is there anything I do or practice in secret?" Now, search what occult practices are and if they are from the devil. Everything God Almighty does is in the light and not the dark. Nothing is done in secret if it is from the God of Heaven. He wants all people to come to Him. There are no secrets involved. That is strictly the devil's territory.

Many things done in secret are meant to deceive and attack us, such as witchcraft. But we have hope. The spoken word and the faith of Jesus are more powerful than any witchcraft or spell. The devil lies and makes you think witchcraft, tarot cards, opening a "third eye," burning sage, Ouija boards, psychics, etc., are powerful. They pull from the power of demons. Inviting demons into your life will only invite destruction, chaos, and sorrow. Using the power of God Almighty invites goodness, patience, kindness, peace, joy, and love into your life. God is more powerful than demons. They flee at the sound of Jesus' name, accompanied by faith. People dabble in the occult because they think they will be powerful. The devil will then destroy their life little by little. He will make them think they are powerful to persuade them to continue the craft. It is all a lie. Examples of occult practices are astrology, witchcraft (Wicca), the black arts, fortune telling, magic (both black and white), Ouija boards, Tarot cards, opening a "third eye," burning sage, necromancy (speaking to the dead), spiritualism, spells, sun/moon worship, incantations, parapsychology, and Satanism. They are all grouped because they are different feathers of the same bird.

People often think they are asking angels

for help while practicing witchcraft, tarot cards, psychics, and even the occult. They are asking angels for help, fallen angels or demons! Remember, demons will collect their fee when they help you. Demons have been around for an extraordinarily long time. They do know things and can help you or guide you. However, you will pay a steep price for their services. The Holy Spirit will also guide you when you trust in Him. But he will repay you with peace, joy, love, patience, kindness, and hope. The Holy Spirit works in conjunction with God and Jesus. Once you trust in Jesus and thank God for sending Him to die for your sins, God will send the Holy Spirit to you. The Holy Spirit helps you by guiding your steps and speaking to you with wisdom. The advice you receive is to help you on this journey, not to kill, steal, and destroy your life.

Seeing in the spirit is not the same as opening your third eye. The third eye is witchcraft. That is divination. Divination is predicting the future or the unknown by supernatural means. It is a sin because we should not ask demons for advice or help of any kind.

You should never have to pay a certain amount for healing or a word from the Holy Spirit. This is how you know if you are dealing with God or the devil. Anyone asking for a certain amount of money for healing, a prophetic word, or deliverance is demonic. They are of the devil if they put a dollar amount on anything. It is different if they are asking for an offering. An offering means you have a choice if you give or not.

Speak this aloud with authority after reading the warning at the beginning of this book:

Any demon that came in through occult practices, I revoke that invitation now. I slam the door on you. I renounce _____(whatever occult practice you participated in: Satan worship, freemasonry, witchcraft, or any secret society). You have no jurisdiction here any longer. I rebuke you, spirit of____ . I command you to leave me now. I bind you up and cast you to the feet of Jesus. I command this right now in the name of Jesus!

Inheritance-Generational

When someone does not overcome something caused by a demon, their children, grandchildren, and the entire bloodline will be destined to fight the same demons that they permitted. This is how some demons enter the womb. A legal right is given to demons to enter the offspring of people they are oppressing.

Someone who is born into poverty will continue down that path because the evil spirit of poverty guides them as well. Someone born to an alcoholic or has alcoholics in their family will be subject to being an alcoholic as well. A person who has sexual promiscuity in their family will also have promiscuity. These are demons with legal rights to be there because their parents never conquered them. We are born looking like our parents' decisions and die looking like our own decisions. Some must fight harder to conquer the demons into which they were born.

There are signs that your family is operating under a generational curse. One sign is that no one in your family can stay married. Many people will live together, not marry, and then break up after their children are born. Children in your family may have their grandparents' or great-grandparents' last names.

Another sign is that many of the men in your family die at an early age. Think about the men in your family. Have any of them died at an early age? Is it more than one? A demon of death may have legal rights over your family.

Another sign is poverty. Poverty is passed down from generation to generation. It is a demon operating in that bloodline. Poverty is a mindset. You have limited information. It is usually accompanied by messiness, alcohol use, drug use, and abuse. These demons work simultaneously together. Addiction also runs in bloodlines. It is a stronghold and is usually accompanied by the demon that causes depression. Many of these demons work together to cause chaos and confusion in a bloodline.

If people do not progress, they live in a pattern or cycle. This is called a stronghold and is meant to keep the person in the same place and addicted. It is a sinkhole in their life that never allows them to move to the next level. Mental illness is also a generational curse. Narcissism, schizophrenia, and bipolar disorder can all be seen running in a family. Demons love to attack the mind. Once they receive access to someone, they have access to that person's descendants.

Demons may have entered your bloodline through witchcraft. If you have someone in your family or your ancestry line who has practiced witchcraft, a demon has a covenant over your family that causes your family to be cursed. Witchcraft is not a lady with a pointy hat and a cauldron. Witchcraft has many faces. Tarot cards, opening a "third eye," burning sage, psychics, Ouija boards, horoscopes, necromancy, mediums, crystals, "lightworkers," and anything called "new age." There is nothing new about the new age. It is an ancient tactic the devil uses to lead people down the wrong path, away from Jesus Christ. It is a game to the devil, but it is unfair to us because we do not know the game's rules. But you can be a curse breaker in your family by speaking the name of Jesus over your entire bloodline.

You were given the rules if you were blessed enough to be born into a real Christian family. The rest of us have had to blindly feel our way through life with trial and error being attacked the whole time. Christian families can break generational curses over their descendants and take authority over these demons who have attempted to destroy their lineage.

I drafted a paper on nature versus nurture in my undergraduate degree program. There is much debate in psychology on whether someone is more influenced by their genetics or the environment in which they were raised. We can shed light on this quickly when we understand demons and generational curses. It is more of a combination of nature and nurture. However, nature plays a more significant role than anyone knew. No matter the environment in which someone is raised, their bloodline is still under a generational curse. Doors their ancestors did not close before they died still have access to that person from their ancestors.

For instance, a person born into a bloodline of poverty will always be in danger of squandering everything they have been given. This is true even if a wealthy family adopted them. A person born under the curse of addiction will be predisposed to that regardless of the environment in which they were raised. If the demon that causes pedophilia has a stronghold on their bloodline, they, too, will have to fight that demon. You can insert any harmful habit in this scenario.

Someone's bloodline plays an integral part in their life. This is true because of demons' legal rights, as discussed earlier. You will be free game for a demon your ancestors did not conquer. People must conquer demons by saying "No." By not agreeing with them, you slam the door in their face. You will be a curse breaker, and that curse will stop with you. Our descendants will not have to deal with those demons when we break the curse.

If we are raised surrounded by Christians and find salvation, those demons must leave. After leaving, they will try to gain entrance again, but the Holy Spirit will help keep them at bay. This is true for anyone. The demons must leave when the Holy Spirit enters. This is the good news of the gospel of Jesus. Praise Jesus!

However, we must realize the truth and understand how to use it. The devil wants to ensure no one understands or believes these truths because he would be finished if they did. I do not want my descendants to fight these dragons because I refused to. If for nothing else, I will do it for them.

Say this aloud with authority.

**Only after reading the warning at the beginning of this book:
Father, reveal all generational curses at work over my bloodline in Jesus' name (Sit and meditate on this for a while. Speak to anything that comes to mind) I take spiritual authority over all generational curses in my bloodline in the name of Jesus. I break all curses, vexes, spells, voodoo, satanic rituals, incantations, and any word curses spoken over me, my family, and my descendants in the name of Jesus. I cover myself and my family**

in the blood of Jesus. Father, I ask you to put your hand and blessing over my family. Place a blessing over all my descendants in Jesus' name. Shower them with favor and all the fruits of the Holy Spirit. I command every unclean spirit on assignment to curse my family and descendants to leave now and never return. The generational curse ends now in Jesus' name. Father, wash every part of me, my children, and my grandchildren in the blood of Jesus. Amen.

If anything came to mind while you were seeking direction from the Holy Spirit regarding any generational curses on your bloodline, speak to those specifically. Some ugly things were revealed when I asked God to reveal generational curses to me. I sat and made a list of them all. (There is a page at the end where you can make your list). I spoke to each one individually. I informed those demons that I am a curse breaker in my bloodline, and their evil plans stop with me!

Unforgiveness

Many people hold onto unforgiveness like a blanket they sleep with at night. Living with unforgiveness is like drinking poison and expecting the other person to die. When someone does something to you that you feel you cannot forgive, it is as if you feel they owe you a debt. When you forgive someone, you cancel that debt. When we forgive someone, it does not mean they are right. It means we want peace that comes with forgiveness. Something most people do not know is that unforgiveness contributes to disease. There are many studies on how unforgiveness contributes to cancer. Do not try to get even, get revenge, or hold a grudge against someone unless you want sickness to chase you down. Speak aloud that you forgive that person and that you cancel their debt.

When you live in unforgiveness, God turns you over to the tormentors. Demons are tormentors and are legal experts. They know when they have a right to enter through unforgiveness. This is a huge stumbling block for people who do not understand the importance of forgiving everyone. Unforgiveness does nothing but torment your life. Unforgiveness will cause bitterness. This bitterness will lead to anger. Anger can and will eventually turn to rage. Rage will keep you from realizing your destiny. It is a slippery slope. You do not realize how not forgiving someone will cripple your spiritual development.

When someone says, "I will never forgive them!" I look at that person with compassion because they do not realize the awful things they are unleashing on their lives by that statement. Forgiveness is critical to salvation.

Say this aloud

Only after reading the warning at the beginning of this book: Lord, I forgive everyone (or speak their name specifically) for _____ in Jesus' name. I cancel their debt. I decree and declare they owe me nothing for mistreating me, shaming me, embarrassing me, cheating me, hurting

me, molesting me, etc. I forgive them now just as I want you to forgive me, Lord Jesus. Father, I ask you to take away all bitterness and help me to forgive those who hurt me. I renounce any need for revenge. I cast the demon of vengeance to the feet of Jesus. I bind you up, demon, and command you to leave me now and never return, in the name of Jesus! Father, wash every part of me in the blood of Jesus. Amen.

Trauma/Abuse

I coupled these together because they go hand in hand. How does it seem fair that demons can come in when you are traumatized or abused? I mean, you did nothing to allow that. The reason this allows demonic oppression or even possession is how you manage the trauma/abuse. If you look up to God for peace, He will keep those demons at bay. Many people will blame God when trauma or abuse happens. This is where the devil will take over. He and his henchmen will take a tough situation and make it worse. They will pay close attention to how you respond to the situation. Any weakness or an inkling of blaming God will result in them destroying you further. Always fix your eyes on Jesus when you are going through a tough situation. Look to Him for peace and even joy through trauma or abuse. "Seek His will in all you do, and He will show you which path to take." (*Proverbs 3:6*). Examples of trauma or abuse: a sudden accident, an unexpected loss of a loved one, being robbed, sexually assaulted, or molested. These are just some examples. We have all seen traumatic situations. These are all things done to you and not by you. If you blame God instead of leaning on Him during these troubled times, you will be hurt, not by God, but by demons. I encourage you to read the book of Job. In the book of Job, the devil took away everything dear to him. He told God that Job would blame him. Job never blamed God, so the devil lost, and God gave Job back much more than he had before. In spiritual warfare, we must cast demons out. Before commanding a demon to leave that entered through trauma/abuse, you must first renounce the situation that caused it to think it was invited.

Say this aloud

Only after reading the warning at the beginning of this book:

Demon that came in through trauma/abuse (you can say specifically what it was), I revoke the invitation in Jesus' name. I take back all the legal rights you think you were given to be here. I look to Jesus for my comfort in these times. I will put my trust in Him to guide me through all hardships in my life. I command you to loose me right now. I rebuke you, bind you up, unclean spirit, and cast you to the feet of Jesus. Father, wash every part of me in the blood of Jesus. In the mighty, precious name of Jesus, I pray. Amen

Ungodly Soul Ties

Any sexual act outside of the sacred bonds of marriage causes an ungodly soul tie. When a person abuses you, it can also cause an ungodly soul tie. This is why victims of abuse have trouble leaving their abusers.

Soul ties invite every demon existing in or around the other person. So, when you have sex with a person outside of the sacred bonds of marriage, you are inviting all their demons to come into your life. Demons only come when they are invited. They pay attention to every move and word we speak.

Imagine a man who does a sexual act with a prostitute. He has allowed every demon that is attached to that prostitute into his life. She has many demons because she has had sex with so many people. If a person has sex outside of their marriage, then they invite all the demons attached to that person into their marriage.

On the flip side of that, what if two people are married as virgins? This is God's plan but do you know why? When two people marry without having invited any demons in from ungodly soul ties, that marriage is untainted. These two people must still fight off attacks from generational or inherited curses. They will both still contend with any demons that were invited through other means. But if two people are saved Christians and marry as virgins, that marriage is most likely going to stand the test of time. Demons will not have legal rights to attack that marriage as they do other marriages.

Demons take full advantage of any invitation we give them. Soul ties can only be broken by forgiving the other person, forgiving yourself, and asking Jesus to forgive you. After doing this with your mouth and heart, you can break the soul ties and command those demons to leave in Jesus' name.

Have you noticed that premarital sex is normalized? How about casual sex with strangers? This is the devil working to spread his demons to the masses. Do you realize when you engage in these activities, they come with unique diseases? Demons or diseases? We must be vigilant and protect ourselves from this deception.

Say this aloud and with authority. Only after reading the warning at the beginning of this book:

I break the ungodly soul ties with
_____ in Jesus' name. Every unclean spirit that came in through the soul ties with _____ ;I command you to leave in the mighty name of Jesus. Father, I ask you to forgive me for the sexual immorality that caused this soul tie. I renounce every connection that was formed. I ask you, Father, to sever any stronghold formed by this activity. I ask you to restore me. Please remove from me anything that came from this connection.
Restore me to the person you intended me to be when you knit me in my mother's womb. Father, wash every part of me in the blood of Jesus. Thank You, Amen.

This can also be said regarding abusive relationships. You can speak this aloud over and over. Ask Father God to fill you with His peace in Jesus' name.

Curses

Our words are immensely powerful. People speak curses over others and themselves. Just by speaking the words over someone can curse them. You do not have to be a practicing witch or Satanist. There is power in the tongue—the power of life and death. A heart and a tongue fighting for the kingdom of heaven are a force to be reckoned with! Curses can also come from practicing witchcraft or the occult. You can curse your entire bloodline by putting your faith in anything related to witchcraft. As previously stated, demons have access to someone related to generational ties. If you have a practicing witch in your family bloodline, there is a good chance that there is a curse over you and your children. The only way to break that curse is by trusting in Jesus to wash you and your descendants clean.

Also, when you speak cuss words or "curse" words, you speak a curse over yourself, the person hearing your words and the person you are speaking the "curse" words about. Have you ever noticed how some people do not like it when these words are spoken in their presence? It is because the Holy Spirit lives in them. The Holy Spirit detests "curse" words. I tell anyone in my presence to stop raping my ears when they speak "curse" words. It is because I know they are speaking a curse over me!

**Say this aloud and with authority.
Only after reading the warning at
the beginning of this book:
I break, bind, and block all word curses
spoken over me and my family in Jesus'
mighty name. I close every door to all
unclean spirits who think they have legal
rights to my life in Jesus' name. Father, I
know every tongue that judges me; You
will condemn it. I renounce and block
any curses my family and ancestors may
have created through witchcraft. I
rebuke all generational curses in the
name of Jesus. If I have ever**

had any dealings with witchcraft, the occult, or false religions, I repent of that now. I renounce it. I sever my ties to this through the blood of Jesus. If I have any occult or witchcraft belongings, I commit to getting rid of them. Please forgive me in Jesus' mighty name. Father, wash every part of me in the blood of Jesus. Amen.

Addictions

It was an addiction that made me realize that there is a God, and He did send His son, Jesus, to die for our sins. So, I have a love/hate relationship with addiction. If I had to walk through that to realize God is real, I would not change a thing.

It felt as though a motor drove me. I had to have alcohol in all my plans. When I would sit down to drink, it was not to relax; it was to get drunk. As I am writing this, I am thinking how I would never have told anyone that horrible fact about myself when I was living it. I can clearly see now what controlled me. I can remember having the thought, "Wouldn't it be cool to be an alcoholic?" I was already an alcoholic when that thought came into my mind, and I had just not admitted it yet. That was most certainly a demon whispering into my ear. I know that now. This is why it is so important to take every thought captive. I wish I had the tools I now have.

Addictions to any drug, including prescription drugs, make you feel that you cannot function without that drug. Everything you think you are doing in secret is known. You chase a feeling you first had when you tried the drug, but you never achieve that feeling. You only destroy your body and mind by pursuing that feeling. That sounds like something a demon would do, doesn't it?

Addictions are not just alcohol and drugs, including prescription drugs. There are also addictions to sex, masturbation, pornography, food, and gambling. Anything you feel that you cannot do without. I know you cannot do without food, but to excess. You will tell yourself you are not addicted, and you can give it up anytime you want. If anyone brings it up, you will get defensive. That is the demons getting angry that you are shining a light into their darkness.

Demons do not want you to realize they are taking control of you. Demons will attack you through any addiction. The demon of addiction wants you to think you are powerless. Once you believe that you are powerless, more demons enter. This is because you agree with them. Once you agree with a demon, it invites other demons.

We must understand that we have absolute authority over these addictions by speaking over them in Jesus' name. Almighty God has created a way for us all to escape the clutches of addiction. All we must do is open the door and accept the gift. These demons do not want you to know the truth, so they will do everything they can to keep you from discovering this fact. They will distract, entertain, and redirect your attention whenever they think you are getting closer to discovering their sinister plans.

The demons that come in through an addiction to pornography spiritually ravage and contaminate your soul. The spirit of perversion, succubus, lust, or incubus spirit will attach to you. The eyes are a lamp to the soul. Whatever you allow into your eyes has access to your soul.

144

A succubus demon will attack a man, and an incubus demon will attack a woman at night. These two spirits will also sabotage your physical relationships. They are jealous and will do what it takes to make sure you do not have a physical relationship with someone in the flesh. The demon will bring jealousy, unforgiveness, anger, and shame to destroy your physical relationships. You will begin to fear that God will not forgive you for the pornography. The plan is to keep you in bondage.

Friend, God will forgive you for anything if you come to Him with true surrender and true repentance. No addiction is too big for Him to overcome.

Demons of addiction cause drug and alcohol abuse. They come to make a fool of you and then destroy your life in the process. They will steal your relationships, your money, your job, your health, your dignity, your family, your beauty, your teeth, and your skin. The demon of addiction watches you destroy your life and laughs at you the entire time. The whole time they are robbing you, they are making you think it is a fun time. You hear thoughts about how much fun it would be to sit and have drinks or drugs. You will say things such as, "It has been a hard week; I deserve some fun," or "Let's celebrate." Everything becomes a reason to "celebrate." You are in a constant wheel of getting drunk or high, being hungover, and doing it all over again. You never get peace. It has been called "having a monkey on your back." It truly is because it never lets your mind rest.

The demon seeks to consume your thoughts from when you wake up until you sleep. You are constantly chasing the next drink or the next high and are never fulfilled at all. You have memories of drinking at a party and having fun. You continue to try to recreate that feeling. But the demon grows increasingly hungry, and it takes more to satisfy him. He is not happy with the amount of alcohol or drugs you took before; he wants more. They call alcohol spirits because that is what they are. They should call them "evil" spirits.

The reason I know addiction is a demon is because I lived with it for so many years. When I finally surrendered to God and the Holy Spirit came to live in me, that demon had to leave. I no longer was a slave to addiction. Jesus said I did not have to live that way anymore. I pray others who are addicted to anything will realize all they have to do is ask Jesus to save them, and they will drop that addiction. It is simple, yet the devil will not let people realize this.

People may think I went from a drunk to a Jesus freak. He saved me from that, and I will serve Him for the rest of my life. I would not return to that life for all the money in the world!

Say this aloud with authority.

Only after reading the warning at the beginning of this book:
I renounce my addiction to _____ in Jesus' name. I turn my back on that addiction and command it loose me now! I rebuke you,
demon of _____ addiction. I bind up every
demon of addiction in Jesus' name. I break every generational curse and ungodly soul tie that invited any demon

to harass me in the name of Jesus. I command every demon causing addiction to _____ to come out now in the mighty name of Jesus. I cast you to the abyss. I command you never to return. Holy Spirit, please come and live in my heart and cleanse me of all unclean spirits in the name of Jesus. Amen.

Fears and Phobias

The spirit of fear and phobias comes through a door opened when something that instills fear happens to you. Watching horror movies will invite the spirit of fear. When something comes along where you choose to be fearful instead of trusting in Jesus, you invite the devil. You can command that spirit to leave once you learn to have faith instead of fear. I told you the story previously about how I now do things that would have once caused me fear. That is because the spirit of fear and so many others left when I was saved. I walk through a dark house, not fearing anything anymore. I walk a fearless, free life. It is the best feeling in this world. Who knew this was what Jesus was all about? The Jesus I used to roll my eyes when someone talked about. The Jesus, I could not give the time of day. I am sad it took me so long to know the truth about Jesus.

**To make the demon of fear leave, say this aloud with authority.
Only after reading the warning at the beginning of this book:**

**"Demon of fear, I command you to loose me right now in the name of Jesus. Demon of fear, I close every door I allowed you to enter. I put my trust in Jesus. I rebuke you, spirit of fear. I command you loose me right now. I bind you up and cast you to the abyss in the mighty name of Jesus.
You have no power here anymore. I have faith over fear. Spirit of_____(name the phobia)**

I command you to leave now in the mighty name of Jesus! I command you never return! I slam the door on you and seal it with the blood of Jesus Christ. Father, I plead the blood of Jesus over my whole body, mind, and soul. Amen."

False Religions

Many people are seeking spiritual enlightenment. In their quest, they stumble upon false religious doctrines. The devil places these in the way of people seeking truth because he wants them to believe they have found truth and stop searching. Any religion that questions the Bible or adds to it, questions the virgin birth of Jesus, the crucifixion of Jesus, Jesus' authority and power of His followers, the sinful nature of all humans, and questions salvation by grace alone are all false religions. This opens doors wide to demons to destroy your life. They will come in through these false religions and wreak havoc in your life. You will feel that you are a spiritual person and not understand why you are being attacked.

New age religion is a way demons will attack you. People are deceived into believing they can worship the earth, moon, and stars. They use crystals and dreamcatchers for protection. New-age people believe in connecting the body, spirit, and soul and reaching enlightenment. These are all parts of the truth; however, if you do not incorporate God, Jesus, and the Holy Spirit, you are communicating with fallen angels who would love nothing more than to destroy you.

Many speak about a spirit guide. These are demons posing as something that is there to help you when truly they are there to hurt you. They should call them spirit misguides. They are not your dead ancestors. That is why it is dangerous to try to communicate with dead loved ones. Demons masquerade as your dear grandmother who passed. They will gain your trust, all while working to see your demise. This is why it is a sin to commit necromancy (speaking to the dead).

God gives us these rules to help us on this journey, not because He is a power-hungry tyrant. He loves us more than we can fathom. He is trying to help us against these evil attacks we take from the enemy. I feel I am trying hard to warn others, but instead, it sounds as if I am judging. I am warning, not judging!

Say this aloud with authority.

Only after reading the warning at the beginning of this book:

Spirit of all false religions, I command you to leave right now in the mighty name of Jesus. I close all the doors you came through. Father, please forgive me for following a false religion. I repent of that now. Spirits who came in through my belief in crystals and worship of the earth, sun, and moon, I rebuke you and command you to loose me right now. I bind you up and cast you into the abyss in the name of Jesus. Wash me in the blood of Jesus from the crown of my head to the soles of my feet. Amen!

Cursed Objects

Cursed objects can be any object used in a ritual to worship a god or goddess. If you hear someone speaking about gods and goddesses, those are demons. These demons are tricky, aren't they? They will do anything to deceive people, just like the serpent did in the garden.

Crystals are harmful in two ways. When we look at crystals for healing and protection, we see them as idols. When we purchase a crystal, that crystal was likely used in a satanic ritual and sold to the masses to bring misfortune to the person who bought it. This is probably not the case if we find a crystal in the earth. God made the crystals; if they were on the earth, they probably would not have been used in a ritual. I did say probably not, with emphasis on probably.

Trusting crystals for protection and healing puts your faith in something other than God Almighty. Not only does it make God's heart sad, but it opens doors to demons.

People who love crystals are adamant about them and get defensive when anything is said about them. Hmm, who whispers those thoughts in their ears? Demons get angry when you shine a light on them.

Objects that may be cursed include dream catchers, crystals, evil eyes, charms, owl statues, Buddha statues, anything with dragons on it, statues of elephants, and angel statues. Pray to God and ask Him what you should remove from your home. He will give you an understanding of what may be in your home, cursing your life.

Satan uses objects as a gate to enter your life to what? Destroy you. Get everything out of your house that may have magic or satanic ties. Cursed objects are the opposite of blessed items. They have demons attached to them. Demons that seek to harm you. Again, I am not judging people for having any of these things. I am warning others. I have researched extensively to find these truths. They are not meant to shed a bad light on anyone. I am simply reporting what I now know to be true.

154

Say aloud with authority.

Only after reading the warning at the beginning of this book:

I take spiritual authority over all unclean spirits in any object in my house in the mighty name of Jesus. I command you to leave right now. This is not a compromise; this is a command. I cast you to the feet of Jesus! Father, wash every part of me and my belongings in the blood of Jesus. Amen.

Cursed Buildings

When people speak of haunted houses, it is not ghosts that are there. It is demons. Demons have legal rights to areas where rituals have taken place or witchcraft. The way to break this curse on the building is to get some olive oil and pray over it. Put some in a smaller bottle to separate it from the rest. You can also touch your belongings with the oil on your hands. *Exodus 40:9* says, "Take the anointing oil and anoint the Tabernacle and all its furnishings to consecrate them and make them holy."

Say this over the oil after putting it in a smaller container:
Father God, thank you for this oil for anointing in Jesus' name. I dedicate this bottle of oil and consecrate it to you, God of heaven. I ask you to place the power of the precious blood of Jesus on this oil. Your blood, Lord, breaks all curses and demonic assignments. It cleanses and destroys all darkness. Through the blood of Jesus, I declare this anointing oil is now redeemed out of the hand of the devil and into the hands of God Almighty. Set this oil aside for God's plans and purposes.
Everywhere this oil touches from this day forward, I ask you to release your power, protection, healing, and divine presence of the Holy Spirit in Jesus' name. Amen

**Dip your finger in the oil and run
your finger along each window seal.
Say aloud:**

**I command all demons in this house to get
out now in Jesus' name. Holy Spirit, I ask
you to fill every inch of this house. Bless
every person who walks into this home.
Lord, build a protection firewall around
my house, allowing only your presence to
dwell within. Let no demonic presence
enter, and may all darkness
flee from this place now. I declare this
home a place of joy, peace, and love in
Jesus' mighty name, Amen.**

Anoint your windows and door seals, leaving the front door to anoint last. Your house will now feel vastly different. I know this because I live in a house considered "haunted." I walked through my house, shouting scripture and commanding all evil that was in the house to get out. This was when I was first saved and had no idea about anything I was doing, but it was right!

When you trust and believe in God, the Holy Spirit guides you this way. I also walked the perimeter of my property. While walking and praying aloud, I drizzled anointing oil on the ground.

Speak any of this spiritual warfare aloud over and over. Keep this book handy and pull it out when the devil rears his ugly head in your   life. Realize you have authority and claim your power!

When you think of demon attacks, you think of invisible beings that will attack you and your surroundings. This is true; however, the devil often inhabits other people and causes them to do his dirty work. Listening to someone with one ear and God with the other is good practice. Use what is called discernment. When I first got saved, I asked in every prayer for discernment. I began to see the world in a hugely different light. It was important to me because I had been deceived for so long. I realized I had lived my whole life with a veil over my eyes and deafness in my ears.

God gives us discernment as a spiritual gift to help us determine if someone is operating from a spirit sent by the devil or by Him. When I was first saved, I wondered how I knew the difference between my voice and the voice of God in my head. I now know there are three voices: my voice, the voice of God, and the voice of the enemy. Life is like walking through a minefield. If you let God guide you, he knows where those mines are and will help you navigate through safely. The enemy places increased mines based on the amount of sin you allow into your life.

When Jesus is talked about with people who have a veil over their eyes and deafness in their ears, they will roll their eyes or begin to not listen to what you are saying. Thoughts like, "This person is crazy" are whispered in their ear. Or their mind wanders away to other things. As I said, if you have read something twice in this book, I deliberately left it in case the demons were distracting you when you read it the first time!

I have always wondered what a testimony is, and now I know. It is the story of how the veil was lifted from your eyes and deafness removed from your ears, and you were allowed to see the truth of our Lord and Savior, Jesus Christ. I also wondered why they called it being saved and why they would say, Jesus, please come into my heart. I make you my Lord and Savior. He literally saves you from this life. I know what the word literally means, and I do mean literally. He steps in and changes your heart's desires. Suddenly, you have your heart's desires because they are different than ever. You see the world very differently. The things that once impressed you seem very trivial. You wonder why you were ever impressed by such things. You realize that you now have power over your environment through Jesus. You can cast out demons, heal the sick, resurrect the dead, and have a heavenly hedge of protection in His name. The name of Jesus is mighty. After you are saved, you have been adopted by God and His kingdom. Then, you are a child of God.

All people are God's creations, but only after you are saved are you God's child. I am tearing up as I write this. These are tears of joy that only come from the Holy Spirit. I also never knew what it was like to cry when my heart was filled with the joy of the Holy Spirit. I understand why people think Christians are sad because they cry. It is the opposite of that! Billy Joel sings about laughing with the sinners instead of crying with the saints. But they do not understand that saints are crying because they have so much joy, peace, and love in their hearts that it brings tears to their eyes. They know their sins and how they do not deserve forgiveness. They are so thankful that it brings tears to their eyes. They would not give that up for the entire world! They know it is better to serve Jesus in a tent than to serve Satan in a castle.

Christians have dominion over their environment. When you say something aloud, you decree and declare it so. Just as speaking terrible things will make them manifest, so will speaking good things and blessings in the name of Jesus. I cannot say enough how powerful the name of Jesus is. When the name of Jesus is on your lips, demons tremble and flee. This is why people make fun of Him and roll their eyes when His name is spoken. Satan is a liar. He wants you to think that Jesus is not cool and that others will make fun of you for saying His name. Jesus is the best thing in this life, and I do not care if anyone thinks He is cool.

Before talking to Jesus, it is important to declare and decree aloud that all voices and spirits not of the Holy Spirit be silenced and cast out in the name of Jesus. This will allow you to hear His voice without the distractions of those devils whispering in your ear.

Devils want to cause chaos, destruction, sorrow, depression, confusion, and all evil things. They like to put thoughts in your head that are not true. Everyone has always said, "Give it to God." That is truer than I ever knew. Talk to God about your problems. He will give you clarity and will guide you. If you listen to the wrong voices that speak to you, they will lead you down the wrong path on purpose. The path that leads to your downfall. They will stand by and laugh at you while you stumble and fall.

I cannot understand why people would invite these spirits into their lives by using witchcraft, psychics, tarot cards, opening a "third eye," burning sage, using a Ouija board, etc. Yes, I do know, the devil has deceived them into thinking they will have power and protection.

Jesus loves you, while the devil hates you and wants to see your demise. Please try hard to understand this. They think they are calling on the power of angels to help them. They are correct;

fallen angels or demons are the ones they are counting on for guidance. When you ask Jesus to save you, understand that you put all your faith in Him, not His angels. Angels of heaven are significant in spiritual warfare; however, ask Jesus to send them. You do not speak directly to the angels.

When you practice witchcraft, you speak directly to fallen angels for help. As I mentioned, they want nothing more than to see your demise. When you invite them in, they are given free rein over your life.

People believe they have a spirit guide, which is a fallen angel or demon. You should not try to communicate with them or speak aloud to them. Instead, you should say to them, "I cast you out in the name of Jesus. I decree and declare spiritual power over my environment in the name of Jesus." Then, say, "I command spiritual confusion upon any spirit that opposes the Holy Spirit."

From the time Jesus saved me, I felt calm in situations I would have previously feared. I used to have a real fear of bees. I recently walked right past a swarm of bees without even batting an eyelash. I was fearful of ziplining and bungee jumping. I did both last weekend. I flew on an airplane near a hurricane with complete peace. I have faith over fear, and it is not just something I say but something I feel. I came upon a wreck on the interstate, and I was the only person to leap out of the car and help the people in the wreck. Two weeks after that, I witnessed a hit-and-run and chased down a lady who ran from the scene! People do these types of things all the time, but not me. So, it is a testament to what the Holy Spirit can do. Am I a superhero with the name of Jesus on my lips and the sword of the Holy Spirit? Hmmm, maybe!

Many things were just "downloaded" to me supernaturally. I knew things that were previously a mystery or had never thought of. I just knew. I once was blind, but now I see! I know it is hard to believe, but here we are.

I did not think anything about angels or demons, but I was told they were constantly battling for our souls! I did not read this somewhere or see a video that spoke on the subject. However, after I knew the truth, I studied everything I could find. I now know God was cultivating a spiritual warrior in me. i put on His armor because i am weak, BUT HE IS STRONG!

Alcohol in Arabic is Al-khul, which means "body-eating spirit." Vodka is a spirit, and Gin is the evil spirit "Jinn." The spiritual realm is hidden from us. They want to work in secret to destroy us all. That demon tricks you into thinking alcohol will make you more sociable, likable, and outgoing. It only makes a fool of us. When you black out, the demon takes complete control over you. That's why you do not remember anything.

I often feel sad that I had to live the way I did for so long. I would not be so passionate now if I had not lived that life. I think of the Rascal Flatts song asking God to bless the broken road. If it took all those things to lead me to the foot of the cross, I would not change a thing.

I pray your heart is stirred to explore the love and forgiveness found with Jesus. It is a powerful journey that is so transformative. If they pursue Him, Jesus will bring hope and purpose to anyone's life. Jesus is a hiding place from this life that kicks us around. Seek His face and watch the demons in your life flee!

Chapter 6

Weapons in This War: The Tongue and The Heart

There is life and death in the tongue. This means the spoken word is so powerful. The enemy only knows what is spoken aloud. Only the Holy Spirit can hear your thoughts. Demons do not know what is in your heart. What is felt in the heart is spoken with the tongue. So, we show our cards to the enemy when we speak. When they hear words spoken, they know what to attack. That is why when you say terrible things about yourself, the enemy will attack using that information.

When you speak badly about someone, the enemy will know how to attack that person. That is why you curse yourself or others when you say terrible things about yourself or others. The Holy Spirit knows what is in your heart, and the enemy does not...until you speak it aloud. When a person speaks something terrible about someone aloud, the devil uses their spirit to attack that person in the spirit realm.

Demons are also experts at your body language. This means they pay close attention to how your body speaks about that situation when you hear something. Using a "poker face" when confronted with information you would typically react badly to is extremely useful. Smiling in bad situations is helpful because it confuses the demons. They will attack you more when you react in an excited, angry, or judgmental way. I also find it helpful to praise Jesus aloud in a challenging situation. Demons cannot stand to hear Jesus being praised, and they will flee.

The devil attacks us so that we will curse God for allowing such a thing to happen to us. After all, we are good people, right? We feel that

God should not have allowed us to be attacked by the devil. We do not want to look at what we may have done or said to invite an attack.

Think of any sin that may come to mind. Now, think of the terrible things that sin invites into your life. If you live in a convicted state (repenting and feeling truly remorseful for sins), you will find that all the problems associated with sin stop haunting you. You begin to live your life with joy and peace. You will never know this way of life until you ask Jesus to save you. The Holy Spirit comes to live in you and helps you stop sinning. This is why asking Jesus to save you with your tongue and heart is so important. The Holy Spirit comes to live in your heart and changes your heart's desires. You become a person that turns their back on sin. Is it to judge others because you do not sin anymore? Absolutely not! When I point out sin in someone, I want them to know what I now know. I want them to understand that they can lay that down by trusting in Jesus.

For twenty years, I went to church and did not totally surrender to Jesus because I thought I would have to stop drinking. The beauty of Jesus is that He did it for me. I did not once try to stop drinking. In my life as a pretend Christian, I would wake up each morning wondering if today I could sit and get drunk. After being saved, I woke up the next day and did not think that. It has been two years now. I still wake up each morning thanking God for the day. That is how I know alcoholism is a demon that only comes to kill, steal, and destroy. When you black out, that demon takes over. That is why you do not remember. That demon will take over and say things you would not have normally said and do things you would not have usually done. This is because the demon has heard you say something private before and knows you are trying to keep it secret. He finds it amusing to tell your secrets while you are drunk. All the while, he is making a fool of you. These are things you allow when you get drunk. You come into agreement with demons. You invite them to destroy your life.

Thank God aloud for things you pray for as if they have already manifested! I now live my life using the knowledge that demons cannot hear my thoughts and only my words and actions. Let me tell you, it is fantastic! I feel like I have a new lease on life. I speak victories, declare blessings, and favor in Jesus' name!

When you wake in the morning, and your thoughts are so clear, it is because the demons do not know what you are thinking. I tried to think of something that would have usually had my mind thinking all kinds of thoughts, but it was silent. All these thoughts were written early in the morning after waking up.

Start every day by decreeing and declaring victory over your day in the name of Jesus. Slay the demons!

Slay Demons

Heavenly Father, I pray against the enemy's attack; I pray against the devil in the name of Jesus Christ. I speak to you, devil, in the name of Jesus Christ; I command every plan that you have against my family and me to be canceled. I come against you in the name of Jesus. I cast out the demon of sickness in the name of Jesus. I rebuke your attempt to make me sick in the name of Jesus. I cast out the spirit of death in

the mighty name of Jesus. I rebuke the plan for the evil you have in my life today in the name of Jesus! I now pray for the warring angels of God in heaven to come before me, stand before me, go before me, and fight for me. For if You are for me, Father, who dares be against me? I now pray for strong angels of heaven to stand guard around my home. I pray against every demonic force that is coming against my family and me. I rebuke them and cast them into the pit. I pray that the warring angels of heaven will smite the demonic spirits that try to come against my family and me. I want any demon who tries to attack my family and me to remember what happened to them in the name of Jesus. I want them to remember they were cast to the feet of Jesus. Father, I pray you will return them to the abyss where they belong. I bind you up, devil, in the name of Jesus Christ for trying to come against me and my family. Every word curse spoken over my family and me I break now in the

name of Jesus. I stand upon the Word of God and through the blood of Jesus. By the power of His name and by the power of His blood, I am victorious in Jesus' name!

We must understand that we are in spiritual warfare every day we open our eyes. This is how we fight! We fight with our tongues, using spoken words. We fight with faith, using our hearts in conjunction with our tongues.

Only Jesus can hear your heart. Demons can only hear your words and know what you look at and listen to. They understand your body language. Thank God aloud for the blessings you want to receive. Speak to Him in your mind to keep demons from listening. When you smile in bad situations, it confuses them.

We have the power of healing and casting out demons in the name of Jesus. The influential, evil people of this world do not want us to know how powerful we are in Jesus' name. If we can cast out demons and heal, then we foil their plans and decrease our need for expensive healthcare. This is detrimental to them because sick people are their cash cows! Let Jesus be your healer by speaking His name over your health issues. I have prayed over a cold or sickness and did not see much of a change, but when I unleash spiritual warfare on a sickness, it leaves quickly.

God sent His Son, Jesus so that we may have a weapon against the demons. We must learn to use it. Once I learned I had the power to tell headaches to leave, I began expanding. I am so bold that I began speaking healing over family members and friends. They began to see that it was true. They would say, "I'm tingling" or "the pain just left." I was speaking to demons while my hand was on my daughter's forehead when she had a fever. She became cooler under my hand. What do you have to lose? Try it; it does not cost a thing!

Let me switch gears. Some people think they can go about their day and sin as they please and then ask Jesus for forgiveness. People say, "Jesus will forgive me for everything I do." While true, He is not a get-out-of-jail-free card. When you commit a sin and repent for it at the feet of Jesus, you must have genuine remorse in your heart and not plan to do it again. The Lord knows what is in your heart. So, He will know if you are not genuinely remorseful and plan to sin again. You are not forgiven for what you are not genuinely remorseful. When I was living enslaved to alcohol, I said the salvation prayer many times, and nothing happened. In my heart, I thought I would have to stop drinking, and I did not know how I would do that. When I finally said it with my mouth and meant it with my heart, he stepped in and took the urge to get drunk.

The key to Jesus's power is faith that it will be done! You can be victorious over the enemy every time if you get out of the things of the world and fix your eyes on Jesus, just like Peter did in the boat. He could walk on the water when he kept his eyes on Jesus but sank when he looked at his circumstances.

I never knew how powerful a heart is. Your heart is truly a thing. I am not talking about the actual organ/muscle. I am talking about the moral compass that guides our decisions. It is enormously vital to protect your heart and the hearts of others. The brain is the thought processor, but the heart is how we feel about that information. It is where beliefs and feelings live. These things are more important than you know. Protect your heart and what you believe with everything in your being. This is where life and death occur. Satan is a deceiver. This is why it is so important to protect what you believe. Once you believe Jesus is Lord, ask him to save you from this life. He died on the cross and was resurrected three days later; your life will be changed. You will walk free like I do!

Since I was saved, I have had no interest in the outer beauty of people; I am only interested in the beauty of their hearts. I want others to see the beauty of my heart. I want others to see the love of Jesus that now lives in me. When someone thinks I am judging them because I point out something that may make them stumble, I do it from a place of love, not judgment. I am not condemning anyone as I walked on the other side for so long. I wish someone would have explained these things to me. I wish someone would have tried to protect me from enemy attacks.

Satan does not want us to know the power we have as saved Christians. He does not want us to know we have so much authority over him and his henchmen. All his plans will be foiled when we step into our authority. We are mighty through the spoken name of Jesus!

Have you ever heard there is power in witchcraft (tarot cards, opening a "third eye," burning sage, psychics, Ouija boards, crystals, etc.)? Sure, you have! I wonder why you have never heard of the power the Holy Spirit has over witches. The Holy Spirit has authority over all demons. Christians have authority over witches by using the authority of the Holy Spirit. That is why witches hate Christians. Satan does not want anyone to know this information and have authority over him and his henchmen.

God and Satan are at war with each other— a war for souls. Demons can influence by coming in through legal rights. A saved person has power over them. You must ask Jesus to save you from this life to become saved. You must confess with your mouth and heart that Jesus is Lord, and He came in the flesh, died, and rose again three days later. But you must believe, in your heart, that he will save you. I asked that a million times in my head and half-heartedly. I was never saved until I cried aloud with my mouth and heart. When you are saved, your entire world changes for the better. All the promises you hear from the church begin to happen in your life. Your heart's desires change in an instant. I have repeated this multiple times, but I want to ensure this is understood. Maybe one of these sentences will slip past the demon's attention, that is keeping you from understanding this!

Take Spiritual Authority

Once I was saved, I just knew I had power over demons by way of Jesus. When I was selling my house, and it was on the market for a while, I had a dream that demons needed to be cast out of the house. I walked through the house, casting them out in the mighty name of Jesus! I carried my Bible and yelled scripture throughout the house. When I came back to the house the next day, I was looking through the back door, and a creaking door sound happened when no door was open. I have no doubt it was a demon leaving because he feared the mighty name of Jesus. No house is "haunted" by ghosts. It is always demons taking on the form of people.

I mentioned the house I live in now. It has been in my family for 45 years and was always said to be haunted. I even experienced things in the house. I once believed wholeheartedly in ghosts. I even named the "ghost" that lived in my house. I called her Pearl. When I realized it was not a ghost but a demon. The spiritual warfare I unleashed made it leave. I walked through the entire house, shouting scripture and casting the demons out in the mighty name of Jesus. I anointed all the windows and all the doors. I commanded all evil spirits to leave my house in the name of Jesus. Demons tremble and flee at the mention of His name. The house feels much better now.

People do not understand the power they have using the name of Jesus. Demons place a veil over the eyes and deafness in the ears of everyone except those saved by Jesus. That is why saved people have discernment that some may call judgmental. They can see the enemy working more than people who are not saved.

When we choose to avoid certain people or situations, it is not to judge them. It is to protect ourselves. Christians have love in their hearts, not feelings of superiority. They love the person but hate the spirit holding that person captive. What is more heart-wrenching to the Christian is knowing that if that person accepted Jesus, those unclean spirits would flee.

There is a kingdom of heaven and a kingdom of hell. Did I already mention this? There truly is fire and crying in hell. Heaven is without pain or sorrow, as demons do not live there. You are content and perfectly loved. This world and everything in it are an exceedingly small part of your existence. It is temporary. The scripture "The meek shall inherit the earth" *(Matthew 5:5)* means that the ones saved by Jesus will be the victors. When Jesus returns to earth, the saved ones will have large mansions and be seated beside Jesus in authority.

All saved people are the body of Christ. This means they are the mouth, feet, hands, etc., of Jesus. They do His work. They help to build the kingdom of heaven. Demons are jealous of people and want them all to go to hell. They are responsible for building the kingdom of hell with as many souls as possible. They're good at it, too: stairway to heaven/highway to hell. Demons wish they had never followed Satan to Earth. They wish they were in heaven with God. The love God has for the people of this earth is unimaginable. He is a gentleman who will never force His way into your life. He gives us free will. This is how the enemy runs rampant in our lives. Once I was saved, I understood how I was attacked. I understand now because I see what has been removed from my heart. All the toxic things were taken away. I still stumble sometimes, but I am convicted when I do. This means I feel a sense of remorse and genuinely want to be forgiven. While God is forgiving, loving, and kind, he will not be mocked! So, do not continually sin and ask for forgiveness for that sin. Sins of this world are not worth burning for eternity. They are just not. I have been told, "I do not know what to believe because there are so many false prophets out there lying to everyone." If you get saved by asking the Holy Spirit to come and save you. Then, you will have a relationship with God, and you can discern and ask God to show you what is from God and what is from the enemy. Read *Ephesians*. It takes 20 minutes and is very insightful on spiritual warfare.

I used to say, "Big man, you'll forgive me for that, right?" I wholeheartedly planned to do it again. Now, when I sin, I am genuinely remorseful and ask for forgiveness. I honestly do not plan to do it again. I even ask for help not to do it again. I want to make God happy. When you fear God, you do not want to disappoint Him. The fear you feel is not a typical type of fear. You have a fear of living without Him.

Someone asked, if God is so good, then why does he allow people to be in car wrecks and die? The way I see it is that we all die, but if an unsaved person and a saved person are in a car wreck and die, that is an unfortunate day for the unsaved person. That is the day they start burning and screaming for eternity. They do not get another chance at salvation. When a saved person dies, that is a day to rejoice because they are entering into the kingdom of heaven. They will live in peace.

Someone said they did not like church because it was a business. I said, "Do not give a dime, but go." But I promise you that you will see miracles happen if you give your first ten percent in Jesus' name!

My house was on the market for three months. I sold my camper for $5000. Before I spent $1, I took $500 to Aldi. I bought groceries for people and told them, "Jesus loves you." I got an offer that afternoon. My real estate agent said I must have called heaven directly that day because God answered in a big way! You cannot out give God. He will give it back to you with interest. You will receive money packed down, shaken, and running over!

Many people want to go to church on Sunday and check the box that it was done. Jesus wants a relationship with you daily instead. It is like a father who is given visitation only. When you are a child, you speak to your father daily, assuming he lives in your house. Your life directly reflects how much influence your father has on it. This is much like Father in heaven. Your life reflects how much influence He has in your life daily.

You have heard that cleanliness is next to godliness, right? The state of your home and belongings mirrors your connection with the Divine. I read this and immediately knew it was true because I used to be the biggest slob I knew. Now, I cannot stand my house being a mess. The Holy Spirit will not dwell where there is a mess. But guess who will? You guessed it: demons. Do not leave your house without making your bed!

When I realized I had power using the name of Jesus, I was reading in my bed. I was reading a book about the power believers in Christ had. When pain would come, I would say, "Spirit of pain, I command you to leave this instance in the name of Jesus!" I would sometimes repeat it a few times. The pain would leave. If I got a headache, I would tell the spirit causing that headache to leave, and it would leave. This was when I began to search for the truth. I began speaking to everything in my life. My family would look at me like I was a crazy person.

My husband came in one day with a look of pain on his face. He said he had a headache. I commanded that headache to leave in Jesus' name. His face was immediately peaceful. I asked him if it left. He opened one eye and said, "Yes." I began dancing around because he thought I was ridiculous the many times I told him it was true. I stopped dancing and said, "The glory goes to God, not me!" I know it is not my power but His.

I have spoken about the power of the tongue and the heart, but I will elaborate. Have you ever gone to church and wondered why everyone stands and sings songs about Jesus in unison at the beginning of the service? That is because there is power when someone speaks passionately about what they are saying. The church service starts with Christians singing in unison because demons will not tolerate being around lovers of Christ speaking His name and expressing their love. If you think one person singing about Him is powerful, imagine how powerful a whole room of saved Christians singing together is!

When Christians engage in spiritual warfare, it is not with weapons of this world. It is with our tongues and hearts! Think of a person in war with one gun alone in the field. When he gets ambushed by the enemy, it is over. Now, think of an army of soldiers with guns blazing. The enemy does not stand a chance. So, once the sermon starts, many demons flee because they cannot stand the environment.

Churches and church leaders do not discuss spiritual warfare because they do not want to upset anyone. However, ignoring that evil spirits exist and are around you all day, every day does not make them go away. When you stand in your authority as a child of God saved by the blood of Jesus Christ, they tremble and flee. According to *Luke 10:19*, we have been given the authority and the ability to trample on snakes and scorpions and overcome all the enemy's powers. Nothing will harm us. Side note: You must be a born-again believer in Christ.

Give in Jesus' name. Give your money, your time, your love. Some people say, "I give all the time." Suppose you give but not in Jesus' name; you serve yourself, not Him. People will say Glory to you instead of Glory to Jesus! When I say, "In Jesus' name," I mean tell someone about Jesus when you give. Speak His name. Also, practice giving your first ten percent in His name. Not after you have paid bills or bought a latte but before you have spent money on anything. Watch what happens!

I realized some things that everyone may already know. Each day is separate from other parts of your life. From the time you open your eyes in the morning until you close your eyes at night. You should praise His name at every opportunity. Because you prayed yesterday, went to church yesterday, gave in His name yesterday, were generous yesterday, and helped someone yesterday, it has absolutely nothing to do with today! This is why it is so important not to go to bed angry. The more genuinely appreciative you are about what you have, the more blessings you will be given.

Every morning is a new opportunity. A new day to praise His most Holy name. A new day of decisions. A new day to live and try to live as close to sin-free as possible. I never realized the importance of each day. Every day is like a lifetime in and of itself. Decisions we make all day, every day, have such an influence on our lives. Our yeses and noes are calculated with each minute. To whom do we give a "yes," and to whom do we give a "no?" A "yes" to God is a "no" to Satan, and vice versa. Our lives are swayed in one direction or the other according to who gets our "yes" and who gets our "no."

I try to help everyone I know, especially family, to know the truth. I often feel like I am standing in a room screaming, but no one can hear me. Evil lurks nearby and whispers in your ear when someone speaks the truth to you. When someone tells you the truth, the evil spirit will bombard your mind with other things so you will not hear it. The spirit may say things such as, "Do not listen to her; she is a Jesus Freak," or "Everyone will make fun of you for believing in Jesus." Or "I wonder what I'm having for lunch." Anything to distract your mind from hearing the truth. Because when you know the truth, you will walk free. Your life will be filled with peace, and your soul will then belong to the kingdom of heaven.

I hope this book helps people struggling through this life. When we take authority over the enemy by speaking the name of Jesus, our lives begin to look a lot different. The devil wants to make sure we never find any of this out. His evil plans would be invalid if we all stepped into our authority and rebuked him and his henchmen. Use this book as a reference and speak to the mountains in your life using the name of Jesus. Experience the peace, joy, patience, and love that only God, Jesus, and the Holy Spirit can bring. Become a victor of your own life!

How to Wield Your Sword

No matter how sharp, a sword is only useful if you know how to wield it. An essential part of the whole armor is the sword of the Holy Spirit, the word of God. When you memorize Bible scripture, you sharpen your sword. You will pull them out during attacks from the enemy. With Bible scriptures on your lips, you will attack the enemy and cut him down.

**Speak this aloud because there is life
in the tongue:
I am the head and not the tail.**

**I will only move upward
and never downward.**

I am blessed when I come in, and I am blessed when I go out. The Lord will cause my enemies who revolt against me to be defeated before me. He causes people to take notice of me in a good way. The right people at the right time. He causes the wrong people to go in the other direction. He causes all things to work together for my good and His glory. He orders my steps and opens doors that no man on this earth can close. He closes the harmful doors and helps me know the difference.

He gives me wisdom because I ask. I have the mind of Christ. I think His thoughts, do His will, and obey His word. I have creative ideas, witty inventions, and problem-solving abilities. He allows me to create wealth and adds no sorrow to it. He creates wealth for me so that I can be generous on every occasion. I thank You, Lord, for being my front and rear guards. Every tongue that rises in judgment against me, I know that You will condemn it. There is no weapon formed against me that shall prosper. You cause even my enemies to be at peace with me. Thank you, Father God, for giving me the right words to say at the right times. I pray You go before me and make the crooked path straight. Thank you for bringing heavenly places to earth. I am walking in the grace and mercy of God. His mercy surrounds me, and His grace follows me. His love follows me everywhere I go. Thank you for all this. Amen, I pray in Jesus name, the Holy Spirit, and almighty God. Amen.

Chapter 7

Secret Powers of Christians

I f you think witches have power, wait until you see what Christians can do! From the time we are born, we are told witches have power by placing spells on people to get what they want. But have you ever heard Christians have even more power?

A witch stopped a Christian and said, "Hey, you're a Christian, aren't you?" The Christian said, "Yes, I am. How did you know?" The witch replied, "You Christians have a light that we witches cannot get. You could take away my power, but I do not fear you." The Christian said, "Why not?" The witch said, "Because you do not know how to use it!" My friend, I have studied since I was saved and compiled these truths of how we can all have power over all the hardships in our lives as Christians.

A woman who was once a witch and was saved by Jesus stated that people would believe her when she told them everything she would do as a witch in the spirit realm. After she was saved, she began to tell them about the power she had as a Christian, and those same people would ignore her or look at her with disbelief. Why is it so easy to believe stories of astral projections, fortune telling, tarot cards, opening a "third eye," burning sage, Ouija boards, spells, and incantations and so challenging to believe the Holy Spirit came to live in you and made all those demons leave that came in through witchcraft? That was a rhetorical question. The answer is that the demons whisper lies into your ears and send distractions.

Christians have power through the faith and blood of Jesus Christ. It is that simple. None of the mixtures, concoctions, or blood sacrifices that witches practice to put a hex on someone. By the way, witches are real, and their number one target is Christians. However, if you implement the methods in this book, you will be protected against their attempts to make you stumble. They are sent on a mission from the devil to foil the plans of Christians.

Witches build the kingdom of hell, while Christians build the kingdom of heaven. However, Christians want to bring love to all, and witches want only to bring self-love to help themselves and get what they want. Many witches operate under hate, loathing, jealousy, evil, anger, and self-importance. Christians operate under love, faith, hope, understanding, and goodwill. The devil cannot stand the fruit of Christians because it is the opposite of what he brings. God wishes to build us up, but the devil only wants to tear us down. If you are praying that something terrible will happen to someone, you are praying to the devil, not the God of heaven, which disgusts the God of heaven.

I believe many witches do not understand that they are operating under the authority of Satan. If you are practicing witchcraft, I beg you to investigate what it is you are doing and from where your power is coming from. It will eventually destroy you and your descendants.

Demons do not fear us because they believe we are uninformed. They think we do not know how to do spiritual warfare, but it is good to show them we certainly do!

Healing

Jesus' ministry consisted of three things. They were healing the sick, casting out demons, and resurrecting the dead. Once you are a born-again Christian, you are given all the powers Jesus had. You can lay hands on the sick and heal them. Every sickness and every disease caused by the enemy must bow down and do what is commanded of them when the name of Jesus is spoken with faith. This is how a believer in Christ can heal sickness. Many times, sickness and disease are caused by a demon who is subject to the name of Jesus. Even more power comes when two or more believers agree to cast out the sickness. Believers in Christ will perform these healing miracles through their faith and by simply speaking the name of Jesus over the sick. Amazingly, God gave us all this power, yet many Christians still do not realize it! If you are a saved Christian, I beg you to start speaking to sickness in your life. The worst thing that can happen is nothing. Remember, I realized I had this power by telling headaches to leave in the name of Jesus. If the headache did not leave, I would still be in the same place as I was. But they left every time! When a headache starts, I say, "Are you sure you want to do that, demon, causing my headache?" It leaves immediately! They fear I will cast them to the feet of Jesus. When a sickness or disease presents itself before me, it is the first defense I go to. I rebuke it, command it to loose me this instance, bind it up, and cast it to the feet of Jesus!

Casting Out Demons

Another word for casting out demons is deliverance. Deliverance means to be set free from demonic oppression or possession. We can be released from the bondage of the devil's attacks. We must have faith in Jesus and know the words to say. That is the purpose of this book. When saved Christians speak these words, they have authority over the demons. Christians are so powerful, but many do not know these truths.

Satan is not God's equal. He is not omnipresent, which means he cannot be everywhere at once. He cannot read what is on your mind. That is why opening your mouth and rebuking the devil aloud is essential. Engage him and command him where to go in the name of Jesus. He must submit! If you do not want the devil to use information to attack you, do not say it aloud.

There are many instances where Jesus cast out demons. He also said we can cast out demons if we believe in Him. Christians often say, "That's not for today". They do not talk about it in many churches. Anytime it is mentioned, it is watered down. Satan has made Christians believe they do not have any power over him. Please understand that this is not the truth. We absolutely have power over him. Does the devil have power? Sure, he does. However, when you invite the Holy Spirit in, you will have power over the devil if you know what to do and say. That is the purpose of this book. The devil has muzzled and bound Christians by making them believe they have no power over him. If you do not believe this, just begin to speak it. You will see it is the truth. What do you have to lose? A crummy, sad life where you always take beatings from an unseen enemy? Try it, and you will see!

Resurrection Power

This one is a little scary and fantastic at the same time. We have been given the power to resurrect the dead! *Ephesians 1:19* says, 19"I also pray that you will understand the incredible greatness of God's power for us who believe in Him. This is the same power 20 that raised Christ from the dead and seated him in the place of honor at God's right hand in the heavenly realms." When we have faith, it can and will move mountains. Command someone to wake from the dead with faith in Jesus and by speaking His name. If anyone reading these words has done this, seen this, or does this after reading these words, please get in touch with me! I want to hear testimonies. I have not personally done or seen this one. The Bible states that we have that power. We must have faith, however.

If people only knew what power they would have through Jesus, the Holy Spirit, and God Almighty, they would swim across a shark-filled ocean to get it.

Things and practices you must do each day to protect yourself and your loved ones:

Speak the Name of Jesus

Have you ever noticed that you could say "God," and no one batted an eye? However, say "Jesus," and people begin twitching and running for the hills. Even people who worship Satan call him "god." That is why it does not bother anyone to say "god." When you speak of the God in heaven, say God Almighty, the God of heaven, the God of Abraham, Isaac, Jacob, Jehovah, and the God of

Moses. Anything that will differentiate Him from other "gods," which are demons.

I cannot say enough how important it is to speak the name of Jesus all day, every day. You do not have to speak the name in front of anyone, but you must speak it. Not when you stump your toe (that's blasphemy). You must ask Jesus with your mouth and heart to protect you from the enemy's fiery darts throughout the day. Demons do not question the existence of Jesus. They know who Jesus is. They tremble and flee at the sound of His name spoken aloud. Have you ever spoken the name of Jesus and watched someone you are talking to get extremely uncomfortable and think of any excuse they can think of to get away from you? That is because their demons cannot and will not listen to the spoken name of Jesus. I know the feeling because it was not long ago that I felt the same way. I find it comical now, however. I speak His name just to see who has "to go now." This is also helpful with discerning spirits. If someone is comfortable speaking about Jesus and seems excited by it, you can pretty much count on the fact that you are talking to a saved person.

On the other hand, if someone you speak to whom you have never met speaks a cuss word as if it were a comma, that person is likely not operating under the guidance of the Holy Spirit. Curse words are like nails on a chalkboard to the Holy Spirit. If He lives in you, you cannot stand to hear them spoken. It is also because, as I discussed earlier, it puts a curse on you.

Armor of God

I have spoken about the importance of the words we speak. Words have power. Just speaking these words lets the spirit realm see you wearing the whole armor of God. Imagine walking out to a battle with no armor. Now, know you have been doing that daily unless you speak this each morning and before bed. We are in a war, and providing ourselves and our families with as much protection as possible is essential. The devil will not go easy on us because we do not know these things. He is relying on it!

You can also put the whole armor of God on your children. Visualize them while also speaking about each part of the armor of God. Speak their name aloud and announce what part of the armor you are placing on them. This is just as important as clothing. You wouldn't send them out with no clothing on, would you? Do not send them into this hateful, vile world without putting the whole armor on them each morning!

Put on the whole armor of God by saying this aloud:

I put on the whole armor of God. I put on every piece of armor from my head to my toe. My helmet of salvation, my breastplate of righteousness, my shield of faith, my sword of the Holy Spirit. I decree and declare my feet will have peace, and my loins will have truth. In Jesus' mighty name!

Plead the Blood of Jesus

Why do we say, "Wash me in the blood of Jesus?" That does not sound clean. In the Old

Testament, people sacrificed an animal to make right the sins they committed. When Jesus was sacrificed, He became the sacrificial lamb for everyone's sins. That whosoever believed in Him would be washed clean by His blood. Everyone who calls on the name of Jesus to save them shall be saved. The catch is that you must mean it!

The blood that was previously from a lamb that was sacrificed for sin is now the blood of a man who came to die for our sins and cleanse all of humanity. Plead the blood of Jesus over everything in your life. When you go to bed at night, pray to God to cover you in the blood of Jesus while you sleep. Ensure your children do this as well. The blood of Jesus protects us from attacks of demons. You may be interested in knowing that lamb's blood is the antidote for a snake bite! It's pretty fitting, considering Jesus (the lamb) washes us clean of all attacks from Satan (the snake).

Father, wash me in the blood of Jesus. I plead the blood of Jesus over myself and my family throughout the day, in Jesus' name.

I put on the full armor and plead the blood before I get out of bed, usually when my eyes open.

Anointing Oil

I keep a dark glass container filled with anointed olive oil at my bedside. Does olive oil have power? No, but I pray over it when I separate it from the big bottle. This makes it anointing oil, and everything it touches will be blessed and protected by the power of the blood of Jesus Christ and the Holy Spirit. My faith is what gives it power. These are weapons the Father has sent us to assist us in combating the powers of evil.

Refer to the cursed building section in this book for information on anointing your home.

Each morning, when you wake up, take a drop of the anointing oil, draw a cross on your forehead, and say this aloud:

Father, I anoint my head with oil. Please protect me from all the attacks of the enemy throughout this day. Protect me with the blood of Jesus. Help me to see the plans you have for my life today. Holy Spirit, be a light for my path and a lamp for my feet. In Jesus' name, I pray. Amen.

In the spirit realm, you will have a large sign of power flashing on your forehead! The demons will flee because they will have no doubt about your faith. After I anoint my forehead, I walk through my house, touching everything in my path, including people or dogs!

Praise and Worship

Do you know what makes demons flee fast? Praising and worshiping God. They will not stand around to hear you praise God, Jesus, or the Holy Spirit. Praise and worship can either be words spoken, singing, or dancing. When you are praising God and speaking the name of Jesus, demons will flee.

Demons operate by placing thoughts designed to make us hate God Almighty or lead us into sin so that they may destroy our lives. They will destroy our lives and make us angry at God for allowing it. If we could silence their voices from whispering in our ears, we could live our lives peacefully. Singing praise and worship songs before asking God an important question is a good idea. If we make those demons flee, they will not try to answer while pretending to be the voice of God. The devil masquerades as an angel of light. Praise Jesus aloud all day to keep the demons at bay.

Pray Over Your Food

Did you know that every time someone cooks you a meal, their emotion goes into the food? Have you ever heard, "It was made with love?" There is more truth in that statement than we knew. If a person prepares a meal for you with good intentions, it will not harm you when you eat it. However, suppose someone cooks the meal while angry at you, and then you eat it?

We are all skeptical of our food sources. We often wonder where our food comes from and what has been done to it before it reaches our plate. For this reason, it is essential to ask God to bless every meal we eat.

Praying over our food in a restaurant is a way to witness to others without even speaking to them. The other people in the room will begin to stir in their hearts. They will think of a time when they used to pray over their food. Maybe they prayed at home with their family as children. They will begin to remember the importance of praying over their food. Maybe they will start to do it themselves because of your example. As Christians, we plant seeds in many ways.

Witches place curses on food for their enemies. I have seen videos of witches in grocery stores putting curses on food. It is true. The curses placed on the food can be anything from a poverty spell to a spell to destroy a marriage to a death spell. I cannot tell you how important it is for you to pray over every meal and drink you put into your mouth. Do not just pray over your food when you think about it. Pray over everything you put in your mouth. It is powerful to break any ill intentions meant for you. Speak the name of Jesus over your food. Simply ask God to bless the food in the name of Jesus. Do not forget to thank Him for the food. Bless the candy if you allow your children to participate in Halloween. However, I implore you to stop letting your children participate in Halloween. Whether you realize it or not, we are all in a spiritual war.

Witches may give a gift of food or anything, for that matter. They will greet you with a smile, seemingly with love and good intentions. The food or the object will have a curse meant to send you into turmoil. This sounds like the poisoned apple in Snow White, doesn't it? Be very discerning when you accept a gift of food from someone. This is also why placing anointing oil on anything you bring into your house is important. However, do not bring anything obviously meant for witchcraft into your house. For example, evil eye, crystals, tarot cards, Ouija boards, etc. Even if you put anointing oil on them and ask to bless them in Jesus' name. Anything about witchcraft should be removed from your house to send a message to the demons that they are not welcome and will not be allowed to stay. Again, they work through legal rights, and those objects give them the right to be there.

I have heard stories of witches cursing food to give the girlfriend of a man they liked. We must be careful of everything we place in our mouth and swallow. We must pray over every bite that enters our mouths.

Fasting

Do you find it interesting that some Bibles do not include *Matthew 17:21*? It is Jesus speaking and saying, "Howbeit this kind goeth not out but by prayer and fasting." That is quoted from the King James version because it is omitted from the NLT version. Check your Bible. It skips from

Matthew 17:20 to Matthew 17:22. The devil wants to ensure we do not find this information.

In *Matthew,* it is about demons. It is unsurprising to realize this part of scripture has been removed from some Bibles. If I were Satan, I would make sure no one saw this bit of information, too! Jesus is giving us a tool to cast these demons out. Christians do not speak of fasting often but should. This scripture is the reason for this: *Matthew 6:16-18* "When you give up eating, do not put on a sad face like the hypocrites. They make their faces look sad to show people they are giving up eating. I tell you the truth: those hypocrites already have their full reward. So, when you give up eating, comb your hair and wash your face. Then people will not know you are giving up eating, but your Father, whom you cannot see, will see you. Your Father sees what is done in secret and will reward you." This refers to when you are fasting. We must speak to each other about fasting. We must discuss how long, how often, and what to do while fasting. It is not to say, "Look at me. I am fasting." It is to teach each other the ins and outs of fasting. It is to let others know of the importance of fasting and prayer. These are weapons in our arsenal that many never even access. Many do not do them because they are unsure about them.

The Bible states that people fast and pray whenever they have a significant decision. If you just fast and do not use the time to get closer to God, it is just a diet. We also become more powerful when we speak the name of Jesus while in a spiritual fast. Demons that would not have normally left become subject to our voices with the name of Jesus on our lips. This is because our faith grows stronger during a spiritual fast. The stronger your faith is, the more powerful you become when speaking the name of Jesus.

The concept of fasting and prayer has slowly become outdated for Christians. We must bring it back to help us in this spiritual war we are in every day. A fast can be one meal or up to forty days! Jesus and Moses both fasted for forty days. If you seek God during your fast, He will make it easier for you. A fast can be with or without water. Before your fast, pray to the Holy Spirit for guidance. The Daniel Fast is fruits, vegetables, and water. You will detox your physical body and spirit when you seek God during your fast. You should fast whenever you make a big decision, when the Holy Spirit urges you to, or multiple times throughout the year.

Read the Bible

Demons cannot stand the word of God. It is the truth, and they are rooted in lies. When we read and study the words of the Bible, they begin to live in our hearts. We speak about the situations in our lives. If you do this, you will see that you are developing wisdom. You will begin to see beautiful changes in your life because a Bible scripture came to your mind when you were in a bad situation.

I previously stated that the Holy Spirit speaks truths into your spirit when you read the Bible. Things that you did not know before are now things you just know. When you seek answers by asking God, the Holy Spirit, and Jesus, you receive answers by an unquestionable knowing. If you watch documentaries about those people who died and went to heaven, they each speak about how they did not talk at all; they communicate telepathically with a knowing.

When you read the Bible, scripture begins to stay in your memory. Memorizing scripture is a powerful tool in the arsenal of Christians. When the enemy comes at you, speaking scripture over the situation will often cause the adversary to retreat. There is power in the word of God. Memorize it and speak to the mountains in your life. Tell them to move in the name of Jesus!

Alone Prayer in a Private Place

What if there was no doubt a God in heaven that you could access anytime you wanted? What would you ask Him? Would you live your life differently knowing He was watching everything? Would you take His advice because He is the all-knowing God? Well, let me tell you something that is the most important thing you will hear. There is a God in heaven, and He loves you so much. He wants us to ask Him questions. He wants us to talk to Him. When we reach out to Him in prayer, He stops everything to listen. He cares deeply for our hearts. He does not care about how much money we make or our education. He only looks at our hearts.

When I say take everything to Him in prayer, I mean everything! If you seek the kingdom of heaven before every decision, He will make your crooked path straight. It seems so simple, but most people will never find this out. Demons make sure we never get truths from God. I told you; the devil wants to make sure we never get the tools from God that will ultimately lead to his demise. The longer you speak to God daily, the closer He will get to you and speak truths into your life. Jesus will save anyone who asks with their mouth and heart. Also, remember to thank God for the prayers He answered. No one deserves a savior, but God forgives all sins when you trust Jesus to save you.

Did you know the devil pleads his case in front of God to destroy your life? He takes all your iniquities to God. He shows Him where you stumble. If God hears nothing from the defense, then He has no choice but to allow the devil to attack related to that sin you allowed. You must genuinely repent when you sin so the devil has no ammunition against you. The devil is called the Accuser. I tell you, friends, plead your case with God. Plead the case of others with God as well. *Zechariah 3:1-2* says, "Then the angel showed me Joshua the high priest standing before the angel of the Lord. The Accuser, Satan, was there at the angel's right hand, making accusations against Joshua.2 And the Lord said to Satan, "I, the Lord, reject your accusations, Satan. Yes, the Lord, who has chosen Jerusalem, rebukes you. This man is like a burning stick that has been snatched from the fire."

God loves it when you lift someone in prayer—pray without ceasing! He wants us to love one another as ourselves, and when you sincerely pray for someone, His heart is filled with love.

Pray Without Ceasing

It is crucial to pray privately so that no one can hear but God. It is of the utmost importance to pray without ceasing. All through the day, seek His guidance. Before deciding to do anything, ask for advice from the Holy Spirit. *Matthew 6:33* says, "But seek first the kingdom of God and His righteousness, and all things will be added unto you." Praying in a private place helps prevent the enemy from overhearing, especially if the devil is influencing someone to listen and interfere. I spoke of monitoring spirits. They will hear your plans and work to lead you down the wrong path. They will make you believe your prayers are being answered, but it will be a lie. When you seek God's face and counsel throughout the day, you will feel bad you have not done it your whole life!

Pray in the Spirit

We, as humans, are made of three things: body, soul, and spirit. *Romans 8:26-27* says, "Likewise the Spirit helps us in our weakness. For we do not know what to pray for as we ought, but the Spirit himself intercedes for us with groanings too deep for words. And he who searches hearts knows what is the mind of the

Spirit, because the Spirit intercedes for the saints according to the will of God." When the Holy Spirit enters a born-again Christian, that person will often receive a prayer language. These are unrecognizable words. I have spoken about how much power we have in our tongues. This language allows us to communicate aloud but privately with God. Demons can only hear what we say. We can speak to God without them knowing what is in our hearts.

The prayer language is different than a prophetic message someone has for the church. That message will be spoken aloud in church and interpreted by a different person.

Your Testimony

When I saw what happened to me once I surrendered to Jesus, I wanted to tell everyone. I discovered that not everyone's testimony is as profound as my story. I wanted everyone to know how I had been going through the motions for twenty years but was not saved until I pleaded with my heart, too.

People often live without much sin taking over when they are saved, and the change is less noticeable, such as people saved as children. I often wish I had been saved as a child, but I would not have the story to tell that I have now.

Everyone who is genuinely saved, however, has a testimony. They know something Jesus brought them out of when they trusted Him. I try to tell people I changed by nothing I did alone. I became a better person. Sadly, some people interpret this as me thinking I am better than them. I cannot figure out how I can think I am better than anyone. I have done some despicable things and confessed them in this book for the whole world to see! Because demons are not in charge of my decisions anymore, I can make better decisions.

Your testimony can silence the voice of the enemy. People cannot dispute if something miraculous happened to you, like what happened to me. It is powerful! Any man can say what they think about God, Jesus, and the Holy Spirit, but I know what's true because I have lived it. Any man can manipulate the truth and misinterpret the Bible, but they cannot shake my faith through what has happened to me. This is why your testimony is so important.

When you have a testimony of what Jesus has done for you, it is essential to share it with others, especially unbelievers. God delivered you from your chains so you can share a testimony with others. You cannot have a testimony without a test. Spread the good news of what Jesus has done for you and can do for anyone who genuinely cries out to Him with their mouth and heart.

Binding and Loosing

This concept confuses people. In *Matthew 18:18,* he spoke of binding and loosing. "₁₈ Truly I say to you, whatever you bind on earth shall be bound in heaven, and whatever you loose on earth shall be loosed in heaven."

Binding tells a demon, "I bind you up, devil of_____." That means he is powerless to attack you. He is wrapped up in a rope. When you loose something, it means to set it free

"Father, loose financial blessings into my life in the name of Jesus." Be sure not to "loose" anything evil. That means you will be letting it run free. However, tell demons to loose you from their grip. Speak to demons in this order and command them to loose you from their grip, rebuke them, bind them up, and cast them to the feet of Jesus. The power in the prayer comes from speaking the name of Jesus. Loose the Holy Spirit's blessing of health, joy, patience, and peace.

Speak this aloud

Only after reading the warning at the beginning of this book:

Spirit of poverty, I command you to loose me from your grip. I rebuke you and bind you up in the name of Jesus. I command every plan you have for my life to become null and void. Spirit of poverty, I cast you to the feet of Jesus. Holy Spirit, I ask you to loose financial blessings over my life.

**Make my storehouse burst at the
seams so that I may be generous
on every occasion in Jesus's
precious name.**

Fruits of the Holy Spirit

When we are saved by surrendering to
God in Jesus' name, He sends the Holy Spirit to
live in us. The Holy Spirit brings fruits and gifts.
Jesus told His disciples that God would send them
a gift. That gift was the Holy Spirit.

The Greek word used for the Holy Spirit
is parakletos. Parakletos means to be called to
one's side. It is translated as advocate, comforter,
counselor, or helper. It is used in the Gospel of
John to refer to the Holy Spirit, whom Jesus
promises to send to his disciples after he returns to
heaven. The Holy Spirit comes to a saved person,
alongside all believers, to provide comfort,
guidance, and assistance. He is a light to our path
and a lamp for our feet (*Psalm 119:105*).

I never understood or realized these
things as a pretend Christian. If I had known
someone would show up to help me live this hard,

burdensome life, I would have said, "Where do I sign up?" long ago.

Love: Agape love is the love we feel when God saves us. We begin to feel love for even strangers. The second most important commandment is loving thy neighbor. When you feel the love of Jesus, you begin to see what this unconditional love is all about. It is a sacrificial, unwavering love. It is giving someone something without expecting them to give you anything in return. You genuinely want others to feel the peace, joy, love, hope, and faith you feel because you love them. These are called "fruits" of the Holy Spirit and are present in all born-again saved Christians. These fruits should be cultivated and nurtured to grow stronger every day.

Peace: The gift of peace, also known as Shalom, from the Holy Spirit helps believers to remain calm in any situation. Does it mean you will be free from conflict in your life? No. It means that when difficult situations arise, you can overcome them and not become so irritated that you can't manage them. In my pretend Christian life, I have heard people speak about "giving it to God." I always thought, "OK, and then what?" I now know that when you give it to God, you will have peace that surpasses all understanding.

Joy: The gift of joy is nothing like I have ever experienced in my pretend Christian life. There can be an aggravating circumstance, but you find joy. I never knew what actual joy was until I got saved. Happiness is a feeling that your circumstances bring. For example, you will feel happy doing something you consider fun. Joy is present even when you are not doing something you enjoy. The Holy Spirit allows you to experience joy in chaos. You will feel happy even when your circumstances look bleak.

Patience: I stated previously that the Holy Spirit brings patience once He enters your heart. You begin to exhibit patience when you were once aggravated and impatient. You begin to tolerate situations that once would have had you raging.

Faith: The shield of Faith is part of the whole armor of God. Having faith in God helps you navigate this life. Your faith shields you from the attacks of the enemy. When you keep your eyes on Him, He will make your crooked path straight. Faith that God exists is the key to your salvation and living eternally in heaven.

Kindness: This is the fruit of the spirit that comes from a culmination of all the others. You become kind to others when you have peace, joy, patience, and love. Agape love allows you to be kind to strangers and loved ones. When you live in the confusion and chaos of the devil's attacks, you cannot help but be mean to others.

Goodness: This can also be seen as a culmination of all the other fruits. The Holy Spirit allows you to exude goodness because you do not readily agree with demons anymore. The Holy Spirit guides our path, and our heart's desires become His. We begin to love others as ourselves. Our decisions are better because the Holy Spirit helps us.

Gentleness: This is the ability to be meek and mild. You find it easy to be kind.

Self-control: The ability to control one's desires and passions, including sexual inclinations. It also includes the ability to control one's anger. Anyone living closely with me in my pretend Christian life can see this fruit of the Holy Spirit in me now.

Gifts of the Holy Spirit

When you are genuinely saved, you receive gifts from the Holy Spirit and experience being baptized in the Holy Spirit. These traits are not given to all born-again Christians. These are meant to help us as we walk in this life to help build the kingdom of heaven. When the Holy Spirit lives inside us, we become new people. I never knew someone would come in to live inside my body, but that is what the Holy Spirit does. He helps to guide your path in this life. I will discuss each of those gifts.

Discernment of the Spirits: The gift of discernment allows the Christian to determine what type of spirit influences a person's actions and words. They can tell if the person is motivated by the Holy Spirit or an unclean spirit. When I was first saved, I prayed to God to give me His eyes so that I could see the way He sees because I had been deceived for so long. I began seeing immediately how people were motivated. I began determining if they spoke of actual or fake love meant to deceive and manipulate. Many people may call Christians judgmental because they try to avoid certain things. Christians avoid certain people or situations for the same reason we avoid snakes. We are not judgmental of that snake; we are simply trying to protect ourselves.

Performing Miracles: Christians can bring forth miracles as in the Bible. With the help of God Almighty, they have the power in Jesus' name. This is a miracle when a demon is cast out, and someone is healed. We must acknowledge Jesus when a miracle occurs and thank Him.

Healing: Christians can cast out demons. Many diseases and conditions are caused by demons seeking to destroy the lives of all humans. When a Christian lays hands on the sick and commands the demon to leave, it must leave. Demons make people think they are not there and are not wreaking havoc on them. However, a faith-filled person can cast demons of sickness out of people.

Knowledge: A part of someone's reality is downloaded to the Christian. They will then know something that is happening in their environment. It may be a person with a disease, a person with a particular problem, or what demon oppresses them.

Wisdom: This is a gift given to prophets. It is the gift of knowing. It can also help guide you on what to do.

Strong Faith is unshakeable faith. This gift is given to someone to help them spread the gospel to others. It usually accompanies someone who has been delivered from a lot.

Speaking in tongues and interpreting someone speaking in tongues: There are two different instances of speaking in tongues. When praying aloud in tongues, the Holy Spirit intercedes for us, as in Romans 8:26, "And the Holy Spirit helps us in our weakness. For example, we do not know what God wants us to pray for. But the Holy Spirit prays for us with groanings that cannot be expressed in words."

The second time speaking in tongues comes into play is when God sends a message to the church. This message is for everyone to hear and is vital for interpretation. 1 Corinthians 14:27 says, "If anyone speaks in a tongue, let there be two or at most three, each in turn, and let one interpret."

When I went to church for twenty years as a pretend Christian, this would freak me out. I would wonder, "What is happening right now?" Someone would speak a different language aloud, and then someone would speak in English aloud. I did not want to look ridiculous by asking. I was a Christian, right? I had no idea what was going on. I know now, and it is so beautiful. I now pray in a prayer language and I am confident I am having a private conversation with the God of heaven. Demons cannot hear or understand why I am petitioning my Father. Surrender to the Holy Spirit, and He will give you this gift! Ask Him to come. Invite Him in with your mouth and heart. You will see what I'm talking about!

Chapter 8

The Power of Agreement

The bible scripture says in *Matthew 18:19*, "I also tell you this: If two of you agree on earth concerning anything you ask, my Father in heaven will do it for you." We do not realize how much power there is when we agree.

When we agree with something bad, it gives legal rights to demons to come in. For example, if we agree to go to a party and get drunk, that puts us one step closer to becoming an alcoholic. A demon will work hard to get you to keep agreeing to that. One day you will wake up and realize you have been an alcoholic for thirty- five years, all because of the first time you agreed to get drunk.

Each journey starts with the first step. That is how a good journey or a bad journey begins. We agree to evil things all the time but do not realize we are handing over our rights to demons. They can only destroy us with our permission. The spirit attached to whatever it is you agreed with.

Think about your life. Is there anything you feel you cannot stop doing? I know the devil tells you lies so that you will say to yourself, "I can give that up anytime I want to. I just do not want to." The truth is you cannot stop because that demon controls your thoughts now. You permitted it by agreeing with it. *Matthew 6:24* says, "No one can serve two masters. Either you will hate the one and love the other, or be devoted to the one and despise the other. You cannot serve both God and money." The master you choose to align with will rule over your life and ultimately determine the fate of your soul.

For instance, if you agree to steal from someone, you give the keys to the demon that is attached to stealing. You will begin to do it increasingly. As I stated earlier, they grow increasingly hungry with each passing day.

When a man and a woman are married, they agree. There is so much power in that union. For this reason, the devil will stop at nothing to drive a wedge between a married couple. He does not want two people living together and coming to an agreement on any matter. A married couple that prays together daily will be unstoppable. That is why the devil always tries to bring strife into a marriage. When the devil comes knocking to attack your marriage, look him square in the eyes and speak spiritual warfare over him. Tell him he will not attack your marriage in Jesus' name. Tell him to get lost. Do not let him divide and conquer. Make your spouse your prayer partner, and watch the devil flee from your lives!

Are you in a marriage where you both are born-again Christians? Have you ever tried to pray aloud together every day? Were you distracted, or did you get into fights? The devil wants to ensure you never step into that power. When two saved Christians stand together shoulder to shoulder in agreement, they are a forceful power. Married couples must be aware and vigilant against anything that tries to wedge them apart. They must understand it is an attack from the enemy.

The tower of Babel, spoken about in the Bible, exemplifies this. It is when Nimrod organized a group of people to build a tower. The tower was supposed to reach the heavens. When he had people working in conjunction with him, God took away their power of agreement. When they descended from the tower, they suddenly began speaking different languages. They could not understand each other and agree.

Many satanic rituals use the power of agreement as a door to enter. The same spirits they make sacrifices to or make a covenant with are the spirits that will torment their children and grandchildren. When you go to a concert and see a satanic ritual and clap, you agree. Your agreement gives that ritual power. When you see something happening and say nothing, you agree with your silence. Look into user agreements. The devil is in the details. You think you agree that the company is providing you with privacy, but that is untrue. If you read the user agreement when it pops up, you will be incredibly surprised by what you read. I do not know many people who read them, but I do. When you agree, you give the person or company rights over you. They will say they can read your texts and emails and see what you look at on your phone for "advertising" purposes.

Think of the Rumpelstiltskin story. He had a lengthy contract. When it was signed, she had signed away her firstborn child. That is how the devil works: trickery. We agree to be tormented. We signed the contract and agreed, right? We are too lazy to read what is in said contract. That is what the devil is counting on. We agreed to the terms and must abide by them.

This is how the devil works. Have you ever heard, "Make a deal with the devil?" I have said so many times that the devil only wants to destroy your dreams. He is sneaky and will make you feel warm and cared for when he rips the rug from under you. This is why reading something before you sign it so important. They intentionally make it long and confusing and do not want you to read it. The devil brings chaos and confusion. It is his specialty. Documents are long and wordy so that you will feel overwhelmed. You just want to get whatever you are signing a document for.

You will create your reality by the words that come from your mouth. Ideas you speak in agreement on will materialize right before your eyes. Sometimes, it is not that obvious. But whatever you agree to in the physical realm will manifest in the spirit realm. I often say the devil does not honor sarcasm. That means whatever comes out of your mouth, the spirit realm hears precisely as it is spoken. Be very careful speaking sarcastically.

I pray you will remember my words the next time you sign your name on the dotted line. I pray that you will seek first the kingdom of heaven.

Chapter 9

When Bad Things Happen
to Obedient People

I could never understand why the enemy is allowed to attack those people who walk in obedience to God Almighty. All of us have all wondered why terrible things happen to good people. Hopefully, this will shed some light on that from a biblical standpoint. The difference between believers and nonbelievers is that believers know beyond any doubt that there is a God in heaven who has tremendous love for us. They know He is always with us. When we surrender to Jesus, He sends His Holy Spirit to live in us. The Holy Spirit sees everything we do and hears everything we say. When a dire circumstance arises be incredibly careful about what you say and do. If you say, "God, why did you let this happen to me?" You will invite more destruction than you initially had. It may be challenging, but we must look to God in these trying times. We need to trust His plan for our lives. Remember, He knows things that we do not know about. If you love Him, all things will eventually work out for your good and His glory. Trust Jesus in all the storms of your life, and you will come out better on the other side. He is a safe hiding place in this challenging life.

Job walked in obedience. The devil told God that if He took away all the blessings from Job, he would curse Him to His face. Job lost seven sons and three daughters, his livestock, and his health. Job kept his eyes on God.

People blame God for what the devil does. We are being tested. Job received twice the blessings he had before because he remained faithful. If we curse God in our valleys, we will only make those valleys deeper and increase the time we must spend there. When you walk in obedience and trouble comes into your life, keep your eyes on Jesus. He will help you weather the trials and tribulations of this life. When you take your eyes off Him during struggles, you will sink in the waves of your circumstances. Do not curse God, whatever you do. He loves us and only wants good for us. It truly saddens His heart when we do not trust Him. When bad things happen to born-again Christians, they have God, who gives them comfort in that time. Seek the kingdom of heaven first, and your crooked path will be made straight. Remember, all things, not some things, work for the good of those who love God.

On the other hand, why do good things happen to bad people? Have you ever seen someone exceedingly sinful yet seem to have everything handed to them on a silver platter instead of consequences for their sinful behavior? In *Proverbs 24:19-20,* it says, "Do not fret because of evildoers; do not envy the wicked. For evil people have no future; the light of the wicked will be snuffed out." Also, *Proverbs 23:17-18* says, "Do not envy sinners, but always continue to fear the Lord. You will be rewarded for this; your hope will not be disappointed." So, we should not feel angry or jealous when we see good things happen to bad people. These people have evil in their hearts and do not know the peace that is Jesus. They do not know true joy or agape love. As I have said previously, gifts from God are more valuable than anything you can buy with money. People who live in sin and revel in it will one day be held accountable for their actions. If we are angry or jealous of them, we invite demons that will attack our lives. We should be praying for them instead of being jealous of them. We should pray that Jesus will find their heart and that they will know His peace and have eternal life when this life is finished.

It is incredibly sad how demons attack and keep people from knowing the truth about Jesus. It is their job to distract everyone from knowing the truth. I pray this world will know the peace, joy, love, and hope you feel when Jesus saves you and writes your name in the Book of Life.

Before I finished this chapter, I prayed to the Holy Spirit to ask if I should add anything. I opened my 1800s KJV bible, and my eyes went to *Proverbs 24:1*: "Be not envious of evil men, neither desire to be with them; For their heart studieth destruction, and mischief." We should not seek the company of evil people. Now that I know how demons attack, I do not want to be around sinful people. I cannot watch the destruction and chaos that surround people comfortable in sin. When around these people, I try to work Jesus into the conversation. They will roll their eyes literally or in their head, but I must tell them what he has done for me.

This chapter was written after my oldest daughter, Kailey, and her husband, Nick, found out they were pregnant. Nick had recently given his life to Christ, and Kailey was already saved. We got the devastating news that the baby had a chromosomal defect called Turner's Syndrome when Kailey was ten weeks pregnant. We also discovered she was a baby girl because Turner's only occurs in girls.

As I had many times before, I began to ponder, "Why do bad things happen to obedient people?" We began to research this syndrome and found that only 1% of babies would make it to birth. As the weeks went on, people would tell her how there were children born with

Turner's Syndrome who were thriving. She began to see pictures of some children who grew up with the problem. Some of the pictures were heart-wrenching. Some stories also came about babies born with the syndrome who made it but died eighteen months later. Kailey and I spent some nights crying on the phone. She did not want her child to be born with all the problems and defects she was seeing. Our hearts were broken.

As she kept growing, Kailey would have awful bouts of nausea. She was also exhausted. The doctor gave her the option of having a medical abortion. She and Nick both told them, "Absolutely not."

After the weeks went by, Kailey and Nick would go for weekly ultrasounds. The baby was getting worse by the week. I began to change my prayers from "Please make this baby healthy and happy" to "Please take this baby home, Father." When they went for their weekly ultrasound at nineteen weeks, she did not have a heartbeat. The baby had passed. This was the answer to what had eventually become my prayer.

Kailey's Poppy was one of the most beloved people in her life. He went to be with Jesus two years ago. I know he was the first one to hold that baby, and that made my heart smile because he was waiting for her when she arrived. Nick wrote the following on Facebook:

"For Georgia Dianne,

She cannot deliver a testimony to you all, so I will do it for her. We found out Kailey was pregnant almost four months ago now. We were very excited as this would be our first-born child. We opted to do the NIPT test so we could know the gender early because we are both very impatient. Unfortunately, we were given the news over the phone that she was at high risk for Turner's Syndrome. Which means one of her DNA strands did not break into two. This is a rare thing that does not happen often.

After research, we understood that our baby girl only had a 1% chance of making it alive to birth, and if she did, she would possibly have some major abnormalities with her organs/body.

Most Turner's Syndrome babies do not make it
past ten weeks.

We were obviously devastated.
But we were not going to give up on her.

Let me tell you.

Every day was filled with prayer, worship music,
anxiety, stress, and sadness.

For the first time in my life, money could not fix
this.
After going through ultrasounds week by week,
we began to understand the complications that
this brings to our child.

Each week began to get worse.

But her heart was still beating strongly.

Every time we went to an ultrasound, we were
nervous, scared, and exhausted. To see an
indication of life on that screen was a feeling I
cannot describe.

I continued to thank Jesus for every week he gave us with our girl. I began to talk about how if He would help her make it through this, I vowed to travel from church to church, delivering the testimony of God's grace.

Our baby girl made it to 19 weeks strong.

The last ultrasound we had was the biggest gut punch I have ever faced in my life.

The biggest pain I have ever felt inside my heart. Quite literally.

But I remembered that our Father in Heaven always has a greater plan for each one of us here on earth. He uses us for things we ultimately sometimes will never understand.

In this season on earth, we have learned the importance of staying faithful to God even in a dark season.

Without God, I don't think I would have made it
through this event in my life.
He has brought me peace in a time I would call
my lowest.

For anyone who has ever struggled with this or is
going through hard times trying to conceive,
let's not forget the Bible story of Abraham and
Sarah.

God's plan is beautiful, even if you don't
understand it. He will not fail you in the end if
you continue to chase Him.

Patience is hard. He is testing us in so many
ways we cannot fathom.

The best news of it all.

She brought me closer to Him.

She taught me more in my life than I could ever
teach her.

Our sweet girl is with our Savior.

Jesus brought her home to His beautiful Kingdom.

I cannot wait to meet you, Georgia.

Georgia, you are MY testimony.
I thank God for everything, even these hard times.

God Bless."

-Nick Geller-

I changed the entire font of this book to "Georgia." You taught our hearts to love Jesus more than we already had. He gave us peace during the storm. I love you, Georgia. I cannot wait to meet you and hold you in my arms when my work on Earth is done.

Conclusion

If you have finished this book, I hope something within these pages speaks to your heart. As I said at the beginning, if this book leads one soul to the foot of the cross, it is worth it. If you want the powers spoken about within these pages, read the salvation prayer aloud at the beginning. Mean it with your heart. Not only will you have power, peace, patience, and self-control, but you will also be a free person! All the bad parts of your life will fall at your feet.

I must tell everyone what Jesus did for me and can do for them. I have seen strange looks, eye rolls, and sighs and heard people saying things about me. I do not care. I only care about what God Almighty thinks about me. It pleases Him, so I will do it! I really cared about what people thought of me in my pretend Christian life. Now, I do not put any weight into what a mere fleshly person thinks about me. I see their eyes roll and hear their sighs. I still pray for them right there. I know who is holding their hearts captive, which gives me great sorrow. I know these things because I lived in an evil captivity for so long.

We should try to understand that we are all victims of demons in our environment. If someone decides to live a life as a homosexual, addict, gluttonous, or anything other than what God Almighty intends for us, I hope they will begin to see it as a demon attack. Am I demonizing these people? Absolutely not. We should all hate the spirit, not the person.

I pray this book gives Christians tools they did not realize they had. I pray they will begin to step into their authority over the enemy. Keep this book handy when you feel that you are being attacked. Open it up and speak spiritual warfare with authority over your environment. Watch demons flee!

I hope that all the readers of this book will seek the heart of Jesus. I pray you all find the peace and joy that I have found. I pray you all realize your power by speaking the name of Jesus. We are more powerful than any witch or warlock, wielding the power of lowly demons. We have the Holy Spirit on our side. He is their ruler. He commands them, and they must listen. I pray you understand that this world is more spiritual than physical. Seek first the kingdom of God and speak Jesus over your life. Watch what happens!

I pray for peace, joy, love, health, and financial blessings for you and your family. I pray Father God be a lamp to your feet and a light to your path. May your storehouses burst at the seams in the unshakable name of Jesus. I pray all the chains of your strongholds be broken in the mighty name of Jesus! Shalom.

Sources

Rebecca Brown, *He Came To Set The Captives Free* (Whitaker House, 1992)

Neil T. Anderson, *The Bondage Breaker* (Harvest et al., 2019)

Derek Prince, *They Shall Expel Demons* Expanded Edition (Chosen Books, 2020)

Frank Hammond & Ida M. Hammond, *Pigs In The Parlor* (Impact et al., 1990)

Alexander Pagani, *The Secrets to Deliverance* (Charisma House, 2018)

John Eckhardt, *Prayers That Rout Demons* (Charisma House 2008)

Frank Hammond, *The Discerning of Spirits* (Impact Christian Books, 2014)

Ron Rhodes, *Spiritual Warfare in the End Times* (Harvest House Publishers, 2021)

David & Jason Benham, *Bold and Broken* (Benham Publishers, 2018)

Priscilla Shirer, *Discerning the Voice of God* (Moody Publishers, 2007)

Nicole Johnson, *Keeping A Princess Heart* (Thomas Nelson, 2017)

Craig McMahon, *Life to Afterlife Death and Back* (2022)

NLT Bible and KJV Bible

Paul C. Schneider-translated by R.H. Charles, *The Books of Enoch* Complete Edition (International Alliance Pro-Publishing, 2012)

Cole Arnold, Ed. D., Ovwigho Caudill Pamela, Ph. D., *Bible Engagement as the Key to Spiritual Growth. A Research Synthesis* (2012)

After Thought

This book's purpose is not to say, "You're an alcoholic" or "You're a drug addict, and you need to stop." This book aims to prove beyond a doubt that Jesus is real and saves us. It is to help others understand the fighting tools Jesus left here so that we can fight back.

As this book was being published, I realized people have different thoughts on what it means to be an alcoholic or an addict. It has nothing to do with how often or the quantity of alcohol you drink. It has only to do with your mind. I only drank 2-3 times a week. However, I could not go past those days without having a drink. Ask yourself this: "Can I go for a week without drinking at all?" or "Can I go for a month without drinking any alcohol?" Insert a drug into those sentences if it is drug addiction. If the answer is "no," you also battle the same demon I battled. Your mind will say, "I have that wedding next week," or "I am going through a tough time right now." That is the demon whispering in your ear to keep you bound in that addiction. When you trust Jesus and step away from that constant bombardment of your mind, you will walk as a free person. You begin to realize that alcohol or drugs are stealing more than they are giving you. Try life with alcohol or drugs in the rearview mirror. It is the best life ever!

List Any Chains of Addiction That You Watched Fall to Your Feet Once You Trusted Jesus

List Any Generational Curses That Came to Mind After Praying

Acknowledgments

I would like to recognize and thank Denesha Degraffenreid. Her obedience to the Holy Spirit helped to bring this book to fruition. She stopped at the plant bus where I was selling houseplants. She stayed around for about an hour and kept buying more things. I asked what she did, and she told me she worked with people who were addicted. I told her my story. A while later, she told me she had written three books. I told her I was working on a book at the time. I told her my book was about what happened to me when I trusted Jesus to save me. I spoke of spiritual warfare; I now realize we are all in daily. She said, "That's it!" I said, "What do you mean?" She said, "The Holy Spirit was nudging me to stay here, and I couldn't understand why. I can introduce you to someone who will help publish your book." I got tears in my eyes because I knew the Holy Spirit gave me the things in this book. I was just being obedient and writing them down. This was a divine encounter that we both knew was true.

About the Author

Kim Irby spent thirty years as a nurse before transitioning out of the field. She holds a bachelor's degree in nursing and a master's degree in healthcare leadership. After experiencing three strokes, she turned to writing as a source of solace and tranquility. Today, Kim co-owns a houseplant business with her daughter and son-in-law. She cares for the plants. With a newfound love for writing, Kim has found a way to channel her creativity and passion into a therapeutic outlet. She credits writing and plant care with bringing her a sense of peace and fulfillment that she never experienced in the high-stress nursing environment.

Kim Irby

Sweetcherryblossomspress@gmail.com

www.ingramcontent.com/pod-product-compliance
Lightning Source LLC
Chambersburg PA
CBHW071714120626
46550CB00001B/236